CIVIL LIBERTY IN SOUTH AFRICA

CIVIL LIBERTY
IN SOUTH AFRICA

EDGAR H. BROOKES

AND

J. B. MACAULAY

CAPE TOWN
OXFORD UNIVERSITY PRESS
LONDON   NEW YORK
1958

Oxford University Press, Amen House, London E.C.4

GLASGOW   NEW YORK   TORONTO   MELBOURNE   WELLINGTON
BOMBAY   CALCUTTA   MADRAS   KARACHI   KUALA LUMPUR
CAPE TOWN   IBADAN   NAIROBI   ACCRA

This study was undertaken on the initiative of the
South African Institute of Race Relations

❦ PRINTED IN THE UNION OF SOUTH AFRICA BY
THE RUSTICA PRESS, PTY., LTD., WYNBERG, CAPE

Preface

This study of civil liberties in the Union of South Africa, prepared on the initiative of the South African Institute of Race Relations, is an attempt to supply the facts about South Africa to those who want to know them. We have tried to do this with a minimum of comment. This is not a polemical book: we leave the facts to speak for themselves.

It would be idle to claim that we have faced our task in an attitude of neutrality, for we believe ardently in that freedom the decline of which in South Africa is the subject of our book; but we have tried to be impartial in the sense of setting out the facts fairly and not making political capital out of them.

We do not claim that this is an exhaustive study. There are discriminatory or restrictive statutes and regulations that are not discussed in this book. The main lines that legislation has followed are, however, enumerated. Laws are constantly being amended and new regulations issued. We have therefore had to fix a terminal date, and the date taken is 31 December 1957. We hope and believe that what follows is a reasonably full and accurate picture of the facts at that date.

Contents

CHAPTER I

Introductory

Civil liberty may be defined as the possession by the individual, within a political community, of those natural rights essential to the free development of personality, under the guarantee of law. By law in this sense is meant accepted legal rules applying equally to all men, left in the hands of the ordinary courts of law, with their characteristic features of publicity, impartiality, objectivity, consistency, and accepted standards of professional ethics. In brief, civil liberty is the rule of law, not the rule of individual Ministers or officials, and it is the rule of law in the sense of basic principles of right, not merely of any and every statute or regulation that has the force, but not the right, of the State behind it. This equating of civil liberty with the rule of law is immensely important: the advocates of civil liberty are not revolutionary protagonists of some new doctrine, but sober citizens defending rights transmitted through their forefathers as being essential to peace, order, and good government.

The freedom that law based on human rights gives man is twofold. In the first place it is freedom for individuals — freedom for every individual within the State, and that without respect of persons, to live a full and normal human life. Political organization of necessity involves some restrictions on the freedom of the individual, if only to protect the freedom of others. Long political experience has, however, enabled us to lay down certain points on which the State should be checked in favour of the individual, and we have learned that so far as these points go the freedom of the individual means strength and not weakness to the State. Such are the rights formulated in the French Declaration of the Rights of Man and in the United Nations Declaration of Human Rights. One of the most striking summaries of these minimum rights is to be found in the so-called 'Bill of Rights' embodied in the first ten amendments to the Constitution of the United States of America, proposed by Congress on 25 September 1789, and ratified in 1791, from which we quote Articles I and IV:

Congress shall make no law respecting an establishment of religion, or prohibiting the free exercise thereof; or abridging the freedom of speech or of the press; or the right of the people peaceably to assemble and to petition the Government for a redress of grievances. . . .

The right of the people to be secure in their persons, houses, papers, and effects, against unreasonable searches and seizures, shall not be violated, and no warrants shall issue, but upon probable cause, supported by oath or affirmation, and particularly describing the place to be searched, and the persons or things to be seized.

Civil liberty extends not only to individuals but to corporate organizations within the body politic—traditionally to the family, the Church, and the University, and also in more modern times to other economic or social groupings. The family, the Church, and the University, in particular, were not erected by the State and cannot rightly be abolished or unduly restricted by it. As Jacques Maritain wrote:

We have to distinguish clearly between the State and the Body Politic. These two do not belong to two diverse categories, but they differ from each other as a part differs from the whole. The *Body Politic* or the *Political Society* is the whole. The *State* is a part, at the summit of this whole. . . . The Body Politic contains in its superior unity the family group, whose essential rights and freedoms are anterior to itself, and a number of other particular societies which proceed from the free initiative of the citizens and should enjoy the largest possible measure of autonomy. Such is the element of pluralism inherent in every true political society. Family, economic, cultural, educational, religious life matter as much as does political life to the very existence and prosperity of the Body Politic. . . . The State is not a kind of collective Superman; the State is but an agency entitled to use power and coercion, and made up of experts or specialists in public order and welfare, an instrument in the service of man. To put man at the service of this instrument is political perversion. . . . Man is by no means for the State. The State is for man.[1]

---

[1] Maritain, *Man and the State* (ed. and trans. O'Sullivan, ch. 1).

As St. Thomas Aquinas put it:

Will, if it is to have the authority of law, must be regulated by reason when it commands. It is in this sense that we should understand the saying that the will of the prince has the force of law. In any other sense the will of the prince becomes an evil rather than law.[1]

Formal statements of this kind may not commend themselves to those nurtured on the British legal and political tradition, which tends to rely on precedent and practice rather than abstract principle, and politically to consider utility rather than any item of natural law. But, although it arrives at the same conclusions by a different path, British tradition is profoundly aware of the dangers of arbitrary State interference, and, however much it stresses the sovereignty of Parliament as a formal principle, does in fact refrain from undue interference with universities or churches, does endeavour to preserve individual rights, and looks with critical disfavour on the growth of official discretion exercised without appeal to the ordinary courts of the land. The British tradition is undoubtedly one of freedom, one in which civil liberty thrives, and although many encroachments have been made on freedom in the course of the widening of the powers of the State to deal with social welfare and technical questions on a scale unparalleled before in history, these encroachments are watched and criticized and have never reached the extent of the inroads into liberty found in South Africa.

British tradition, while it most powerfully affected the British colonies of the Cape of Good Hope and Natal, was also influential in the republics of the Orange Free State and, to some extent, the Transvaal. We have here, however, also a tradition indigenous to the early republican to consider. Politically this was very markedly one of rugged individualism, such as might be expected in any frontier society. The Transvaal, in particular, was a community made up of men who were little inclined to obey cheerfully even laws within the undoubted sphere of the State. As Bryce truly says of the powers of the earliest republican constitutions, 'They would have liked to get on without any government, and were resolved to have as

[1] *Summa Theologica*, Qu. 90, Art. 1.

little as possible'.[1] The Volksraad of the Orange Free State
was prohibited by the Constitution from making any law
restricting the right of public meeting and petition, and this
provision of the Constitution could be amended only by
majorities of three-fifths of the Volksraad in two successive
sessions. Article 19 of the earliest Transvaal Constitution
granted the liberty of the press. Bryce says that the absence of
any formal Bill of Rights was due, in part at any rate, to the
assumption 'that the Government would be a weak one,
unable to encroach on the rights of private citizens'.[1]

It may be claimed, however, that the principle of the rule
of law was never so fully established in the Transvaal as in its
sister republic. Calvinistic authoritarianism among a people
whose situation bore much resemblance to that of the Chosen
People in the wilderness may have played a part. Nevertheless,
until the closing years of the Kruger regime a sincere attempt
was made, as far as frontier conditions permitted, to ensure the
supremacy of the law over arbitrary decisions. With the
opening of the Witwatersrand gold-mines and the problems
arising from the influx of the 'Uitlanders', elementary rights
such as those of freedom of association, of the press, and of
public meeting were seriously interfered with, and the dismissal
of Chief Justice Kotzé by the President symbolized the growing
power of the Executive as against the courts. Thus it may be
argued that the later Transvaal practice departed sharply
both from the British and from the earlier Voortrekker and
contemporary Free State respect for law.

Even if all this be *fully* admitted, the change from what has
historically been the dominant tradition of the greater part of
South Africa to the present state of affairs seems to call for
explanation.

No doubt it is mainly due to the fact of colour in South
Africa. The non-Europeans, too backward and after their
conquest too submissive to require such extensive legislation
in earlier years, have, as they have grown in education, in
maturity, and in political ambition, and as they have been
influenced by the proposed changes since 1945 in the outside
world, been subjected to more and more legislative and adminis-

[1] Bryce, 'Two South African Constitutions', *Studies in History and Jurisprudence*, vol. 1.

trative restriction. It is impossible to exaggerate the effect of
the colour question on the limiting of civil liberty in the Union.
Colour differentiation and the subjection of the coloured races
were a part of the republican tradition, fully as much as civil
liberties were. To preserve the one principle the upholders of
republican ideals have sacrificed the other; but, as will be
indicated in more detail later, restrictions on the freedom of
the non-whites have inevitably brought in their train great
and increasing restrictions on the freedom of the whites.

Certain other conditions have also changed. From 1652 to
the days of the Great Trek, 'Government' to the frontier Boer
was always the rule of foreign officials—the Dutch East India
Company, the Batavian Republic, the British. It was natural
to resist Government. And even when republican independence was attained officials were largely drawn from the Cape
Colony or from Holland and not from the republican farming
community itself. The role of the 'Hollander' officials in the
old South African Republic is well known. Not so well known
is the fact that of the eight senior officials who stood by President Steyn to the bitter end, not less than six had English or
Scottish names.[1] After the war, the Milner officials were introduced, and it was largely they who headed the government
departments at the time of Union. Not until the late 1920's
did the public service begin to lose its distinctively English-
speaking character. Only in 1948 was there set up a government
which was wholly Afrikaans-speaking.

As step by step the authorities of the State ceased to be
thought of as foreigners, the strong opposition to governmental
interference gradually lessened. Nationalism was stronger than
individualism. Trust in the leaders of the national struggle
and the fear of colour gradually destroyed the strong principles
and traditions of individual freedom and the rule of law. It is
this that explains why, in spite of strong traditions to the
contrary, civil liberty has been steadily reduced in South Africa
in recent years, beginning certainly before 1948 but most
markedly after that year. The object of this book is to present,
as objectively as possible, the facts of this decline of liberty.

It must not be thought that any attention paid in this

[1] N. J. van der Merwe, *Marthinus Theunis Steyn*, vol. 2, ch. 1. It is not, of course,
suggested that they were recent importations.

chapter to political theory is a mere academic flourish. For the
house of liberty in the Union did not begin to fall until after the
foundations had been undermined. The political battle was
won in the schools and universities of the Union before it was
won at the polling-booths and in Parliament. British political
ideas had influenced thought even in the republics before the
unhappy war of 1899–1902, and they continued to do so even
after it. But the new nationalism was disposed to turn from
British conceptions precisely because they were British and to
be influenced by authoritarian continental theories because
they were not British; nor could it escape the contagion of
Nazi thought during the early 1930's when so many minds in
so many countries felt the evil fascination of a theory of which
they were to be ashamed when its essential wickedness was
more fully exposed. It is important to remember that the rule
of law that many tend to defend, because it is one of the best
traditions of Britain, is weakened in its hold on many South
Africans by that very defence. Such are the intellectual
problems of a country of many races and many antipathies.

Because the most extreme forms of State control and authoritarianism are to be found in laws affecting the Africans, it is
right to examine yet a third tradition of South Africa—the
African or Bantu tradition. It is argued by some that since
the Africans are used to despotic rule under their own chiefs
they can have no grievance at despotic rule under government
officials and Ministers. This argument ignores the whole senti-
ment of nationalism, as if it made no difference to the African
whether he was ruled by his hereditary chief or by a white
official. But what is more to the point is that the Bantu tradition
is not one of despotism. The defenders of authoritarian rule
quote Shaka. But Shaka, famous though this military despot is
among the Zulu people, was no more typical of Bantu rule than
was Mussolini or Hitler of the politics of western Europe. Bantu
chieftaincy was as much like the kingship of medieval Europe as
makes no matter.[1] Monarchy was certainly the ideal of the
Middle Ages, but it was limited monarchy. It was limited, in
the first place, because it was under the law, a customary law
based on the morality of the people. Legislation, whether in

---

[1] Except that the Bantu king was, like the Roman king, also a priest.

medieval England or in eighteenth-century Zululand, was exceptional. The experience that the Bantu faces at present of a stream of new laws and regulations, with new criminal sanctions, year by year, is something wholly foreign to his tradition.

A Bantu chief was limited, further, by the presence around him of his uncles, his headmen and other counsellors. Like a medieval king he reached his decisions only after consulting his 'great men', and the decisions were very rarely in conflict with the feeling of his great men. These great men in their turn were in touch with the older and more reputable men among the mass of the people, and so a rude system of consultation was built up, which, if not democracy as we understand it, was not mere authoritarianism.

And in the last resort the people, too, were consulted: occasionally as before a declaration of war by a formal tribal gathering; always through the pressures which they knew how to bring. Incipient despotism could be checked by secession of the discontented; in the last resort it was tempered by assassination.[1] The counsellors, living among the people, were aware of the currents of thought, the sullenness and the rising discontent against unpopular policies, in a way in which no white official could be. All these facts tempered any authoritarian tendencies in the Bantu form of government and introduced into it some rude elements of democracy. To impose upon them today a stream of legislative enactments, alien to their past laws, on which they have never been consulted, and opposition to which on the part of chiefs, counsellors, and people is in vain, is to introduce a wholly alien system; while to do it in the name of African tribal tradition from which in any case tens of thousands have broken away is indeed to add insult to injury.

The arbitrary powers given to the Governor-General as Supreme Chief[2] arose from a device adopted in Natal in 1849, based on the exceptional case of Shaka, and only resorted to as a means of overcoming the scruples of a legalistic 'Recorder'

[1] Even the all-powerful Shaka lost by the secession of Mzilikazi the people who gave their name ultimately to Matabeleland in Southern Rhodesia; and he was later assassinated by his own brothers, Dingane and Umhlangana.
[2] See Chapter XII.

of that time. By the Native Administration Act of 1927 these powers were extended beyond Natal to the provinces of the Transvaal and the Orange Free State, and by an amending Act of 1956 to the Cape.

In an exceptionally able protest, dated at Bloemfontein, 6 April 1928, a convention of paramount chiefs and chiefs of the Union stated: 'Shaka's government was a form of government contrary to Bantu system', and, the document continues, 'if it is the policy of the Government that the Bantu people should be governed by their own law and customs, we feel it our duty as guardians of our people, to point out that this should be in accordance with Native Law and not with the wishes of the White race.'[1]

Thus the third main stream of South African tradition is also against administrative despotism. The attack on Bantu freedom under the law is against their own political conceptions and experience. But there is another important point to be borne in mind. It is that legislation against the African has gradually, but surely, undermined the liberty of the white man, by making South Africa accustomed to arbitrary decisions, administrative tribunals, and the lack of consultation. Although in general the restrictions on white South Africans are far less than those on the African population, they are much greater than they were ten years ago, and a study of the succeeding chapters will show what inroads have indeed been made into the liberties of the white community.

Since the most striking of the statutes restricting liberty have been enacted since 1948, some may argue that the year 1948 is the 'great divide' in the process of encroachment upon freedom. As one studies the details of this process, it is an inevitable consequence of the facts that most of the references are to laws and events subsequent to that date. This nettle must be grasped. It would be very unfortunate for a study of this kind even to give the impression of being an attack on a particular political party. But the facts must be faced. The Cabinet of 1948 was the first in the Union's history to contain no members deeply committed to the British tradition with its stress on the rule of law. The fear of colour, the feeling that apartheid must be

---

[1] Cited in Brookes, *The Colour Problems of South Africa* (Lovedale, 1934), pp. 106–7.

1

carried out by any means however drastic, the trust reposed
by the white electorate in the men whom they had put in
office so that they have been ready to see civil liberty sacrificed
for national ideals, all explain this tendency. To deny it would
be to evade the facts. At the same time, it must not be imagined
for one moment that restrictions on civil liberty began in 1948
or are the monopoly of one political party. Long before that
date South Africa experienced that trend towards bureaucracy caused by the development of the Welfare State that
was to be found in every modern country. Moreover the process
of legislating differentially on questions of colour, and diminishing individual rights in the process, had perhaps begun as
early as the Natives Land Act of 1913 and certainly as early as
the original Natives (Urban Areas) Act of 1923, although the
men responsible for that enactment could hardly foresee the
lengths to which its many amending acts would go. The
Native Administration Act of 1927 took long strides in the
direction of leaving the rule of Native areas to official discretion,
unhampered by the control of the courts of law. The Riotous
Assemblies and Criminal Law Amendment Act of 1930 introduced some very questionable new principles into South
Africa's public law. The Asiatic Land Tenure and Indian
Representation Act of 1946 might be regarded as a step
towards the demarcation of 'group areas' by law. No South
African government of whatever party has been guiltless of
encroachment on civil rights.

During the war years (1939–45) extensive powers were given
by Parliament to the government. In face of the deadly peril
to which even far-off South Africa was exposed, especially after
the fall of France in 1940, the need for this strengthening of the
executive power can be understood. Even the system of intern-
ment, which quite undoubtedly involved some grave personal
injustices, could be defended in general terms as necessary.
But, the atmosphere of multiracial South Africa being what it
is, it is understandable that the spectacle of white men, some of
them good Afrikaners, being arrested and imprisoned without
trial by a proper court of law strengthened the feeling that the
same process could be applied to black men without any
special wickedness, or at least placed a specious argument in
the hands of those who were willing to do so. True, it was

something like martial law in time of peace, but many men were able to justify it by taking the internments of the war years as a text, or pretext.

It will appear from the preceding paragraphs that it is not possible to fix 1948 as the year in which encroachments on liberty began in South Africa, nor to fix responsibility for such encroachment on one political party only. Yet in a sense 1948 is a 'great divide', particularly since there are four fields in which there is little to be said before that date and much after. These four fields are the Church, the University, the sanctity of freehold title to land, and the special position of the police force.

Curiously enough it is the Church, the attack on which has aroused the most attention, regarding which this contrast between the years before and after 1948, is least clear-cut. The Natives (Urban Areas) Consolidation Act of 1945, by giving the Minister of Native Affairs the power to prohibit the erection of churches intended mainly for Africans in urban areas not being locations or Native villages, did not shock the conscience of Christians as much as the later attempts (1957) to make all attendance of Africans at 'mixed' services subject to the permission of the Minister, or at least to give him the power to ban such attendance in specific cases; but, however deplorable the later developments, it would seem that the principle was admitted in 1945. The attempt to introduce university apartheid, and to set up non-European university colleges run not as academically free bodies but as Departmental institutions under strict control, was novel and revolutionary in character. Moreover, before 1948 it was the invariable custom, when circumstances necessitated or were thought to necessitate the movement of groups of Africans from their homes, to provide them in their new homes with the same type of tenure as they enjoyed in their old ones—freehold for freehold. On more than one occasion since 1948 this just policy has not been followed, and indeed it is today the policy not to give Africans any new freehold rights even in cases of transfer of population. This encroachment on property rights, to which relatively little attention has been given, is a very serious inroad into liberty. The greatest apologist for natural rights, John Locke, would assuredly not have regarded it as a small matter.

Finally there is the question of the police. As this is handled in Chapter III, there is no need to go into detail here; but there can be no question that not only have the statutory powers of the police been significantly increased but also the way in which they have used even the legal powers that they previously had has led to a considerable increase of restrictions on freedom. Moreover, individual cases have recurred, not habitually but with disturbing frequency, of individual policemen arrogating to themselves powers beyond those conferred on them by law, as if a police officer *qua* police officer possessed powers other than those entrusted to him by law.

To stress overmuch the fact that many of the most striking encroachments on freedom have occurred during the last decade does, however, expose us to the danger of underrating the growth of bureaucracy before 1948. There has not been a sufficiently strong and alert opposition in South Africa to the growth of official discretion as such. Bureaucracy, as its opponents like to call it, is often defended because the new powers granted are in the hands of a government acceptable to ourselves. Governments change but the extensive powers remain and form the precedents for new encroachments. There is something a little inconsistent in being shocked at powers taken by a government in 1948, but complacent about powers taken in 1945. Those who feel for civil liberty must surely accept the obligation to defend it from encroachments by their political friends, no less than by their political enemies. This study will, it is hoped, deal with civil liberty in South Africa on the merits of the case. It is hardly possible to enumerate in this book *all* encroachments on civil liberty in South Africa, but an honest endeavour has been made to deal with all the more important ones. A digest of all laws affecting liberty, or —to take a different case—of all laws specially or differentially affecting non-Europeans for good or bad, would be very useful. This book does not claim to be such a digest, but it does set out to give the salient facts about civil liberties in the Union in as objective a manner as possible.

CHAPTER II

The Rule of Law in South Africa

The classic exposition of the principle of the rule of law is still to be found in A. V. Dicey's *Law of the Constitution*. According to him the principle involves the following: firstly, that 'no man is punishable or can be lawfully made to suffer in body or goods except for a distinct breach of law established in the ordinary legal manner before the ordinary Courts of the land'; secondly, that every man is subject to ordinary law administered by the ordinary tribunals; and thirdly, that the general rules of constitutional law spring from the ordinary law of the land. The principle common to all three meanings is the supremacy of law, ordinary law as between person and person, over every form of executive action.

Modern writers on public administration have criticized Dicey's exposition as not corresponding to the facts even in Great Britain itself, the *fons et origo* of the principle. They claim that men are in fact punished by administrative tribunals, appeal from whose decisions to the ordinary courts is often specifically excluded by Acts of Parliament, that this development is inevitable in the modern Welfare State, and that statute has established many specific rules governing the relationship between individuals and administrative officials.

That this process has been going on in Great Britain is incontestable, and we need not take time here to consider whether it is beneficial or harmful, or whether it could or could not have been avoided. The point must be accepted that any study of the working of the present British Constitution must involve the modification up to a point of Dicey's exposition of the rule of law.

But the critics must not be allowed to carry us too far. If it is true that administrative tribunals exist and do inflict punishment on citizens, it is also true that they do not in fact deal with the more serious or more personal offences, and do not ever, at any rate in peacetime, impose the most drastic forms of punishment, such as death or a long term of imprisonment. If it is true that every man is subject to administrative laws, it is also true that the ordinary law of the land is still clearly in the superior position. If it is true that in certain fields there do exist rules of constitutional law that have no affinity with the ordinary law of the land, it is also true that on most of the really fundamental issues the connexion is maintained.

It is well that it is so. For a complete and direct negative to each of Dicey's three points would mean that liberty secured by law had ceased to exist, and that such small freedoms as emerged in practice would be merely the result of the benevolent exercise of discretion by a despotic government. Englishmen who have accepted without much opposition (though not without grumbling) the great extension of administrative discretion during the past few decades would have been up in arms had the fundamentals of freedom been touched. The abolition of the rule of law means despotism—benevolent or malevolent, but still despotism. No point is better established in political science than the proposition that civil liberty depends on the rule of law; and the abrogation of the principle of the rule of law would mean the end of civil liberty as we have known it.

The position in Great Britain is, thus, that the principle of the rule of law still exists, and that, though many intrusions have been made on it in the way of uncontrolled administrative discretion, it is still the prevailing principle of the Constitution. In South Africa the position is that while the rule of law is still the basic principle, the exceptions made by statute are so far-reaching and so numerous that it can no longer be said to be *in practice* the prevailing element in the nation's life.

It is for subsequent chapters to indicate, in more detail than is possible here, how far this process of legislative erosion has gone; but some points need to be made now.

There is a real connexion between civil liberty and the right to vote, clearly distinguishable from each other though these conceptions are. When so much of man's life is governed by statute (and by subordinate legislation such as proclamations and regulations) as is the case today, the retention of civil liberty depends in great measure on the watchfulness of Parliament, and when the citizen has no vote, a great safeguard for the maintenance of the principle of the rule of law disappears. This is the principal justification for the inclusion in this volume of a full study of the franchise (see Chapter XI). Particularly does this argument hold good when the unenfranchised belong to particular racial groups that are regarded as inferior and discriminated against as such (see Chapters IV and XII). So far-reaching is this discrimination in Union statute law as to raise the question whether racial distinction has become fundamental in South African law, a question raised in Chapter IV.

Fundamental to the classic conception of the rule of law is the principle that in the end public officials, however exalted, are in the eyes of the law mere ordinary men who have no inherent rights but only such rights as statute law and undoubted common law gives them. 'A colonial governor, a secretary of state, a military officer, and all subordinates, though carrying out the commands of their official superiors, are as responsible for any act which the law does not authorise as is any private and unofficial person.'[1]

Experience in the totalitarian states of Europe during the present century has shown very clearly that the most vulnerable point in the armour of freedom is the position of the police force. Restrictions on the right of the police to make domiciliary visits, to arrest without warrant, or to exercise other drastic powers, hamper authoritarian government, even when Ministers and permanent public servants are given extensive powers. It is to be noted that in the penultimate stage of movements towards communist totalitarianism the communists hold almost invariably in the last tottering coalition government the portfolios of the Interior and of Justice; having these, they can control elections and the police, to whom are then given unlimited powers to arrest political opponents. It would be a gross exaggeration to say that the South African police force was an Ogpu or a Gestapo, or that South Africa had become wholly a police state; but the rise in the powers of the police has been disquieting and there are disturbing indications of new trends in the interpretation of their functions. These matters are further considered in Chapter III. It is important

---

[1] Dicey, *Law of the Constitution*, ch. 4.

neither to ignore these changes nor to exaggerate them, and they will be handled as a matter of careful legal inquiry in this spirit.

The setting-up of administrative courts is not peculiar to South Africa: Great Britain has many of them, too many as some think. But in the Union these courts are not only numerous; they are far-reaching in their powers, affecting the life of the citizen in a way in which no administrative courts affect the life of the citizen in Great Britain. These administrative courts (with, it is true in the first case quoted, a limited appeal to the ordinary courts) affect the racial classification of citizens, a factor all-important in a country where so many differentiations are made on racial lines; and (without any appeal to the ordinary courts) where he may live and carry on his business; and, in the case of anyone whose political opinions can in any way be deemed communist, in the specially wide statutory sense given to that word by Act 44 of 1950, section 1(i), (ii), and (iii), how and when and where he may express his political opinions. It will thus be of use to study the relevant provisions of the Population Registration Act, the Group Areas Act, and the Suppression of Communism Act.

The Population Registration Act (No. 30 of 1950) provides that every person shall be classified by the Director of Census as a white person, a coloured person, or a Native, as the case may be, and every coloured person and every Native shall be classified by the Director of Census according to the ethnic or other sub-group to which he belongs.[1] The term *Director* is defined as including the Assistant Director and any officer acting under a delegation from or under the control or direction of the Director.[2]

Among the effects of this classification are the following: A person claiming to be and passing as white but classified as coloured will be liable to have his name removed from the general voters' roll and put on a special coloured voters' roll;[3] to be required to vacate his house in a European area and to live in a coloured area; and most poignant of all, to have to move his children from a European school and put them among children with whom they have in the past been prevented from

---

[1] Sec. 5.   [2] Sec. 1(iv).
[3] See Chapter XI.

associating and whom too often they have been taught to consider as inferior, with psychological results on the child which
in the atmosphere of South Africa might be of a far-reaching
character. Another distasteful effect is that section 11(1) opens
the door to one's neighbour's objecting to one's classification
as a white man, which in South African conditions may well
give great power to a malicious neighbour and encourage a
vicious form of witch-hunt.

A person claiming to be and passing as coloured but classified
as Native will be liable to be ordered to live in a location or
Native village, to carry a pass or similar document, to lose all
rights of domicile in the town where he lives (unless born and
continuously resident there), and to be held up by any police
constable for production of pass or tax receipt.

These are only some of many disadvantages accruing from
a classification downwards in the racial scale, and this classification is in the first instance entrusted not even to an administrative court but to a single administrative officer who may
delegate his power to a subordinate.

From the decision of the Director (or his subordinate) an
appeal lies to an administrative court.[1] In the original Act the
aggrieved person was allowed to appeal at any time, but by
amending Act, No. 71 of 1956, section 1, this appeal to the
administrative court must be made within thirty days after the
classification becomes known to him. Moreover, he is required
to submit affidavits for which any but a well-educated
person will require legal assistance.[2]

The administrative court is a board of not less than three
persons including the chairman, appointed by the Minister,
and presided over by a person, appointed by the Minister,
who is or has been a judge of the Supreme Court or a magistrate.[3] Thus the composition of the court is entirely in the
Minister's hands and it may consist entirely of civil servants.

From this court an appeal lies to the Supreme Court, but
the appeal must be lodged within thirty days after the decision
of the court.[4] The appeal may be taken further to the Appellate
Division of the Supreme Court.

When one considers the ignorance and poverty of many of

[1] Act 30 of 1950, sec. 11.   [2] Ib., sec. 11(2).
[3] Ib., sec. 11(3).   [4] Ib., sec. 11(7) to (10).

the people affected, it is easy to see that the need to act within a very short time, the onerous conditions, the need for legal costs (which may be very heavy in both the first and the subsequent appeal)—it is easy to see that all these requirements mean that the decision of an administrative official may often in fact be final.

This decision, while the social and legal structure of South Africa is what it is, may damn not only a man but all his descendants after him, for if a man is classified as 'coloured' under the Population Registration Act, great though perhaps not absolutely insuperable difficulties stand in the way of any of his descendants before they may ever be recognized as white.[1] It is a terrific power to be vested in a civil servant.

The operation of the Population Registration Act is well illustrated by the case of *Goliath* v. *Director of Census & another*,[2] in which the finding of the Race Classification Appeal Board was set aside. The Board had assumed—incorrectly in the view of the Court—that the onus was on Goliath to disprove the Director of Census's classification, not on the Director to prove it.[3] Goliath was generally accepted as a coloured person, lived in a coloured community, and served in their local advisory committee, and his children attended coloured schools. He was reclassified by the Director of Census as a Native (*a*) because he looked like one, and (*b*) because his mother's name was Molamo; and this notwithstanding the fact that both his parents were coloured persons whose home language was Afrikaans. All his associations had been with coloured persons. Had there been no appeal from the decision of the administrative authorities, Goliath would have been subjected to all the disabilities under which an African (as compared with a coloured man) suffers, and his children would have been compelled to attend African schools, probably using the Sotho language and not Afrikaans as their medium of instruction.

---

[1] If there is a continuous process of classifying based on census returns made every so many years, it is possible that a child born after the initial classification may have a right to challenge his own classification when that is advertised under sec. 8(2) of the Act. It would be difficult for him to be reclassified, but perhaps not impossible.

[2] 1956 (3) S.A. 95 (T), especially at 100-1.

[3] The onus was changed by an amending Act as a result of this decision.

The Group Areas Act originally became law as Act No. 41 of 1950. Since then it has been amended several times and finally reissued with amendments as a Consolidated Act, No. 77 of 1957. Any references made here are references to the Consolidated Act.

To describe the provisions and effects of the Group Areas Act in full would require a whole chapter, or indeed a small treatise. We are concerned with it here mainly as an illustration of the way in which vital personal rights are decided by administrative courts instead of the ordinary courts of the land. It is sufficient to say that under the Group Areas Act individuals may, on the ground of race only, be restricted in the ownership of property to certain areas of a town and excluded from all other areas, may be compelled to live in certain areas and no other areas, and may be compelled to vacate businesses legally built up in certain areas, losing business goodwill, and establish them (if they wish to continue in business) in other areas. A man may be prevented from living in a house that has been lawfully built by him before the passing of the Group Areas Act, and a son may be ineligible to inherit a property lawfully acquired by his father. The operation of the Act may entail economic ruin for an individual or for a whole group of individuals. In these circumstances it would appear that the ordinary courts should, in all fairness, be open to persons who consider themselves aggrieved.

Powers are given under this Act to the Governor-General,[1] the Minister of the Interior,[2] and, by delegation in certain cases, the Chairman of the Group Areas Board.[3] It is true that after 1965 (by which time surely most of the group areas will have been proclaimed) resolutions of both Houses of Parliament will be required before the proclamation of group areas,[4] but this is not so now, nor will it be so for some years. A proclamation may be made by the Governor-General 'whenever it is deemed expedient'.[5] The issue of permits is made by the Minister 'in his discretion'.[6] Thus the only grounds of appeal to the courts would be the allegation of mala fides on the part

---

[1] *Inter alia*, Act 77 of 1957, secs. 14, 15, 16, 20, 21, 22 and 23.
[2] *Inter alia*, ib., secs. 16, 18, and 34.   [3] Ib., sec. 19.
[4] Ib., sec. 20(3).   [5] Ib., secs. 20 and 21.
[6] Ib., sec. 18.

of the Governor-General or the Minister, or the contention—a difficult one to establish—that the decisions were so outrageously inequitable or impracticable as to show that the Governor-General or the Minister had not applied his mind to the matter. Moreover, the provisions of section 41(4) of the Act operate in favour of the executive power. They are quoted in full:

Whenever in any proceedings under this Act or any law repealed by this Act, whether civil or criminal, it is alleged by or on behalf of the Minister or any officer in charge of a deeds registry or in any indictment or charge—

(a) that any person was at any time an Asiatic in terms of any law repealed by the Group Areas Act, 1950 (Act No. 41 of 1950); or

(b) that a company was at any time a company wherein a controlling interest was held by or on behalf of or in the interest of an Asiatic in terms of any law repealed by the Group Areas Act, 1950; or

(c) that a person is or at any relevant time was a member of any group; or

(d) that a company is or at any time was a company wherein a controlling interest is or was held by or on behalf of or in the interests of a member of any group,

the allegation shall be presumed to be correct unless the contrary is proved.

The authority vested in the Governor-General, or the Minister, under this Act, is exercised on the basis of reports made by the Group Areas Board, which may be considered as a subordinate administrative court. It consists of not more than twelve members appointed by the Minister. A member may be removed from office on the ground of incapacity or misbehaviour, but only by the Minister. Members are appointed for such periods, not exceeding five years, as may be determined by the Minister at the time of their appointment. The Minister, in consultation with the Minister of Finance, shall determine the remuneration and allowances that each member may receive. The Minister appoints the chairman and vice-chairman. No qualifications are laid down for chairman, vice-chairman, or members. Members need not have had any previous legal training.

Nowhere in the Act is there any principle laid down that

non-Europeans shall be allotted the less desirable parts of a town, or a less area per head of population, or be subjected to losses disproportionate to those inflicted on Europeans. The Minister on the introduction of the original Bill gave assurances that it would be administered equitably, and the Act has been defended as a measure merely for racial separation and not in itself inequitable before the General Assembly of the United Nations. It must be assumed therefore that if an effective appeal had been left to the ordinary courts of the land, any Determination under the Act would have had to conform to the principle 'separate but equal'. As it is, in no Determination made up to date have non-Europeans been given an area equal in proportion to population to that given to the Europeans; in no Determination have their losses been proportionately equal to or less than the losses inflicted on Europeans. The Act has thus operated in every instance to the detriment of the non-European. In other words, had the Act laid down that its object was a penal one, it would have been grossly unjust and inhuman but perhaps not a matter for discussion under the heading, The Rule of Law in South Africa. Enacted, however, as it has been, in terms of studied moderation, as if its object were simply to separate the races, not to penalize them, and advocated by the Minister who introduced it as a measure which would be applied reasonably and humanely, it stands as a classic example of what can be done by administrative courts using a procedure quasi-judicial but freed from all true judicial qualities and cut off from the healthy main stream of judicial decision.

It may here be noted that the Board declined to hear the Transvaal Indian Congress as representing members who were affected by its proposals, but was corrected on review.[1]

In the case of *Sader & others* v. *The Natal Committee Group Areas Board & another*,[2] the Court felt itself compelled by the wording of the statute to agree that the Natal Committee could competently sit in judgment on proposals drawn up by itself.[3]

In only a few cases have the proposals put forward under the Group Areas Act resulted in a final Determination, but the

---

[1] *Transvaal Indian Congress* v. *Land Tenure Advisory Board*, 1955 (1) S.A. 85.
[2] 1957 (2) S.A. 300.
[3] The Chairman's explanations, quoted at 302 E–H, should be read.

recent proclamation of group areas in Johannesburg has given a rude shock not only to those immediately concerned but even to average white opinion as represented by the Johannesburg City Council. Briefly, the proposals are to move a mass of Indians from Vrededorp and other areas in the middle of Johannesburg to Lenasia, about eighteen miles from Johannesburg and outside the municipal boundary. In one street, seventy shops with stocks of nearly £1,000,000, goodwill of £100,000, and real estate and equipment worth £150,000 are affected. The coloured people, too, are being moved. Newspapers have emphasized the case of the coloured man whose father was a burgher of the Republic and his mother a St. Helena woman, and who fought with the Boer forces at Ladysmith. He now has to leave the home for which he paid £5,000 and in which he has lived for twenty years. It is inconceivable that a true court of law (but alas! the intervention of such courts has been ousted by the Act) would have accepted the transfer of the Johannesburg Indians to Lenasia as an honest attempt at separation without any other motive. For obviously the effect will be to ruin the Indians as traders and force them to find other types of employment, despite the fact that virtually all employment in the government service and much outside it is closed to them.

In most of the Transvaal towns the Group Areas have not been proclaimed but the proclamation in Johannesburg has aroused apprehension and indeed real fear as to the smaller centres. For the Group Areas Act has had the effect of encouraging municipalities to come forward with the most inequitable and inhumane proposals, embarrassing even to the administrative court concerned. Even if these are not accepted, the result is likely to be a compromise between them and a really equitable separation. The working-out of this process may be studied in the village of Lydenburg. All the Indian stores are in one and the same street, except one, which is in leased premises, the lease being due to be terminated at the end of the present year in any case. Segregation already exists, therefore, and the proposed objects of the Act are already attained. There are only two stands in this *de facto* Indian area owned by whites, and both owners are willing to sell. Notwithstanding all this, the Town Council first planned to move all the Indians two and a quarter miles out, some distance from any road. The Group Areas Board itself called for more equitable proposals. A Reference and Planning Committee (merely a department of the Board itself) later suggested that the Indians be moved about one mile, out to the north; while the Town Council's revised plan is that they should be moved half a mile out of town, to the east across the river. Both these 'moderate' and 'compromise' proposals have the same effect as the first outrageous one—to move the Indian traders right out of the shopping area.

Similarly at Nelspruit, the Indians are already segregated within the village proper, only two stands being owned by whites in the area in which they live. The Town Council has proposed that all the Indians should be moved either to the west of the town, almost three-quarters of a mile away, across the railway line, or to the south-east, two and a half miles from the town and a quarter of a mile from the nearest main road. Here the effect would be the same—to drive the Indians out of the commercial centre and ruin their businesses. It is needless to say that this is not the object of the Group Areas Act as defended before the General Assembly of the United Nations or even in our own Parliament. One is free to choose between two explanations: either that the intentions of the government are being thwarted by its own administrative courts, from which no appeal lies to the courts of justice properly so called, or that the government is tolerating through its administrative courts the execution of a policy that it has been ashamed to avow in public because of its indefensible lack of equity and human consideration. There is no third explanation possible: the choice lies between these two.

The Suppression of Communism Act (No. 44 of 1950) has as its object the restriction of the dissemination of doctrines which may well be regarded as not only false but dangerous. Nevertheless the methods it has adopted are in direct opposition to those of the rule of law. The determination of whether a man is a communist or not is removed from the ordinary courts of the land and left to the decision of the Governor-General. The penalties thereafter inflicted upon him are also purely matters of administrative discretion, that is, by the Minister of Justice or 'an officer designated from time to time by the

Minister',[1] or a 'committee consisting of three persons appointed by the Minister, of whom one shall be a magistrate of a rank not lower than the rank of senior magistrate'.[2]

While the jurisdiction of the courts is not formally removed, the wording of the Act is such that on most (though not all) points there is no possibility of a successful appeal to them. The Act is studded with such phrases as 'is deemed by the Governor-General',[3] 'if the Governor-General is satisfied',[4] 'the Minister may require',[5] 'whenever in the opinion of the Minister',[6] or 'whenever the Minister is satisfied'.[7]

A communist is defined as

a person who professes to be a communist or who, after having been given a reasonable opportunity of making such representations as he considers necessary, is deemed by the Governor-General or, in the case of an inhabitant of the territory of South West Africa, by the Administrator of the said Territory, to be a communist on the ground that he is advocating, advising, defending or encouraging or has at any time after the date of commencement of this Act advocated, advised, defended or encouraged the achievement of any of the objects of communism or any act or omission which is calculated to further the achievement of any such object.[8]

If we strip this clause down to its essential meaning, what it says is that 'a communist is a person who is deemed by the Governor-General to be a communist'.

A person so deemed, or a person who is a member of any organization which the Governor-General is satisfied is propagating the principles or promoting the spread of communism or furthering the achievement of *any of the objects of communism*,[9] may be required to resign as a member of either House of Parliament or of a provincial council or of the Legislative Assembly of South West Africa, and not again to become such a member,[10] and any person falling under the same

[1] Act 44 of 1950, sec. 8(1).   [2] Ib., sec. 17.   [3] Ib., sec. 1(i)(iii).
[4] Ib., secs. 2 and 6.   [5] Ib., sec. 5.   [6] Ib., sec. 9.
[7] Ib., sec. 10.   [8] Ib., sec. 1(i)(iii).
[9] Ib., sec. 2(2). The italics are ours. *Query*: Might not the achievement of full racial equality in the Union be regarded as 'one of the objects of communism' even if it is held by non-communist or anti-communist organizations?
[10] Act 44 of 1950, sec. 5(1). A report from a committee of the Senate (in the case of senators) or of the House of Assembly in the case of all others concerned is required; but under our Constitution the Minister could hardly be Minister unless he had a majority of the House of Assembly behind him.

definition may be prevented from being a candidate for any of the legislative bodies specified.[1]

The Minister may, by pure executive order, remove any such person, irrespective of whether he has been convicted of failing to observe the Minister's previous order or not, from his place of residence,[2] and prevent him from entering any other specified area for an indefinite period[3] (which, incidentally, may gravely affect his professional or business career), and may also prevent him from being a member of any specified organization.[4]

Many further powers are vested in the Minister under the Act, for example the prohibition of certain public meetings,[5] but these will be dealt with under their proper heads in later chapters. It is sufficient to note here that almost every power given is given in such terms as to oust the jurisdiction of the ordinary courts, that where matters do go before the courts certain presumptions are, by the Act and its amending Act of 1954, required to be made by the court for the Crown and against the individual concerned,[6] and that nearly all such relief as the courts were able to afford individuals in the first four years after the passing of the Act was removed by an amending statute.[7]

A very important illustration of the growing tendency to take away administrative action, especially as it concerns Africans, from the jurisdiction of the ordinary courts of the land is afforded by the Natives (Prohibition of Interdicts) Act, No. 64 of 1956. It is true that by section 5 of the Act its provisions are to be applied by Proclamation to specific cases, and not to all cases. Proclamations 79 and 283 of 1957 have applied it to several classes of action, but not to all. Section 2 of this Act is quoted in full:

Whenever any native is or has at any time prior to the commencement of this Act been required by any order—

(a) to vacate, to depart or withdraw from, to be ejected or removed from, not to return to, not to be in or not to enter, any place or area; or

---

[1] Act 15 of 1954, sec. 4.   [2] Act 44 of 1950, sec. 10(1).
[3] Ib., sec. 10(1).   [4] Ib., sec. 5.
[5] Ib., sec. 9.
[6] e.g. ib., sec. 12; Act 15 of 1954, sec. 5.
[7] Act 15 of 1954. See especially sec. 11.

2

(b) to be removed from any place or area to any other place or area; or

(c) to be arrested or detained for the purpose of his removal or ejectment from any place or area,

no interdict or other legal process shall issue for the stay or suspension of the execution of such order or the removal of the property of such native in pursuance of such order, and no appeal against, or review proceedings in respect of, such order or any conviction or finding upon which such order is based, shall have the effect of staying or suspending the execution of such order or such removal in pursuance thereof.

The Act even goes so far as to cancel interdicts already granted.[1] It is true that the courts may ultimately declare the order invalid and even award compensation to the person concerned,[2] but in the meantime he has been put to the loss and inconvenience of the removal, and his right to appeal to the courts of his country for interim protection has been withdrawn.

It is noteworthy that this Act applies to Africans only.

In conclusion, attention should be drawn to the Public Safety Act, No. 3 of 1953. It virtually abrogates the function of Parliament and the courts in placing the power to suspend these, in certain circumstances, in the hands of the Governor-General, i.e. in effect the Executive. Contrary to the practice of similar statutes elsewhere, no time limit is imposed to guard against the Executive's assuming these vast powers when the need is not present.

We come now to sum up the position. Whether or not we agree with the principle of the rule of law, we must agree that immense inroads have been made into it in South Africa especially (though by no means solely) during recent years. It may be that some do not care or do not feel that the principle of the rule of law is worth supporting. It may be that some who uphold that principle in theory feel, not without sorrow, that the special circumstances of South Africa demand its partial sacrifice. Be that as it may, the fact remains that the rule of law has in fact been challenged extensively on points that affect intimately the lives of thousands of citizens. That fact cannot be challenged.

---

[1] Act 64 of 1956, sec. 3.   [2] Ib., sec. 4.

But we would go further. In our judgment the principle of the rule of law is fundamental to freedom, and freedom is fundamental to the good life. No special circumstances can justify the abrogation, in time of peace and for an indefinite period, of so many freedoms. Liberty involves the rule of law. Men must be ruled, but good government leaves them essentially free. Tyranny involves the rule of men rather than the rule of law, and official discretion in the hands of men intoxicated with power liberates them from the control of law and leads to tyranny. Some official discretion there must be, and properly exercised it may well be beneficial. But the wider its bounds are set, the more it touches the fundamental rights of human beings; and the less it is subject to the safeguard of appeals to impartial courts, the more baneful it becomes. In South Africa it has got out of hand, and is like a cancer growing in the body politic, feeding on the healthy tissues.

The matter is fundamentally one of principle, whatever the race of the individual concerned. Yet when it is considered that the officials who give the rulings are all Europeans, the case of the non-Europeans, and especially of the Africans, is hard. Almost the whole of the African's life is now governed by administrative decisions, appeal from which to the courts has been deliberately denied by Parliament. There is thus not merely the tendency of the Administration to stand by its men against outsiders, but the terrible pride of race, the urgent need that the white man should not 'lose face' by being put in the wrong before the black man. Gone are the days of the *Sigcau* case, when the Chief Justice, Sir Henry de Villiers, could uphold a Pondo chief against the arbitrary actions of the most influential English South African of his day, Cecil John Rhodes, Prime Minister of the Cape and ruler of half the hinterland. In most cases of the *Sigcau* type today, no appeal would lie to our admittedly still just and fearless courts. There may be some melancholy pride in being bullied by a prime minister, but none in being bullied by a second-grade clerk or a policeman. These are the thousand petty tyrants who really rule the Africans today, and it requires quite extraordinary fearlessness on the part of their superior officers to tell the black man that wrong has been done to him, that the wrongdoer has been reprimanded, and that the wrong will be fully put right. We speak not without some knowledge of what goes on in this dark administrative underworld. Often, it is true, the offender is privately reprimanded, and sometimes justice is done in a decorous way that does not expose the offending officer. This is something, though it does not exalt justice as justice should be exalted; but even this is not attained in many cases, and the poor are bullied and oppressed by men who have been given powers that few men are fit to exercise over others and that none ought to exercise without there being the opportunity of appeal to a competent court.

Oppression and official control are not synonymous. Laws may be oppressive even if they leave no discretion to officials. Officials can be, and sometimes are, kindly and just within the limits left them by higher authority. But the saying 'all power corrupts and absolute power corrupts absolutely' has much truth in it. And the system of leaving fundamental rights to official discretion is inherently wrong as contrasted with the protection afforded by true courts.

Courts of law operate in public. The individual has the chance, through a trained legal practitioner, to have his case put well and clearly. Any witness giving evidence hostile to him can be cross-examined. Charges against him must be clearly formulated and adequately proved. The judgment given will be objective, based on the facts, and consistent with previous judgments in the same field.

Contrast with this the decisions of officials. They take place behind closed doors. The sufferer often does not know really what the accusation against him is. He has no chance of hearing or cross-examining those who provide evidence against him. There is not the slightest guarantee of consistency. Too often the prosecutor is judge in his own case. Those who make the decisions are themselves servants of the government, which can dismiss them, transfer them, or withhold promotion from them, if their decisions are not what the government wants.

True it is that one of the greatest needs is for better human beings. Even in a system inherently unjust, the just and kind man can do much to mitigate hardships and resist repression. Nevertheless the protection of the poorest individual against all the might of Government by impartial courts of law is one of the highest achievements of that Western civilization of which we in South Africa proclaim ourselves in a special manner the defenders. Love is greater than law always and at all times, and courts of law are to love as moonlight is to full sunlight. Yet what a moonlight it is, how clear and soft and even beautiful are its cold rays, and how much better it is than the Stygian darkness of administrative tyranny!

> *To live by law*
> *Acting the law we live by without fear*
> *And because right is right to follow right*
> *Were wisdom in the scorn of consequence.*

How much misery and oppression of the helpless and despised could be avoided in South Africa if men were penalized only by trained judicial officers, only for clearly defined and adequately proved offences, and only after a fair hearing. But this which should be the rule of life has become in our country, especially so far as the African people are concerned, the exception.

CHAPTER III

Status and Character of the
Police Force: increased and special powers

The general functions of the police force in the Union were recently the subject of judicial decision when Rumpff, J., held that these functions arose *ex virtute officii* and involved the duty to protect the internal security of the State, the public peace, and to prevent offences.[1]

It is important to observe that the function of preserving the internal security of the Union was specifically linked in the judgment with the obligation of preventing crimes which threatened that security.[2] In that respect this particular function is merely a part of the general duty of the police to keep watch and ward and to prevent the commission of crime. Apart from that it has no sanction. Halsbury put it this way:

> The most important general duties of constables are to preserve the King's peace and with that object to keep watch and ward in their several districts and to bring criminals to Justice. As part of his general duty to preserve the King's peace it is the duty of a constable to prevent breaches of the peace and the commission of offences; and if he has reasonable grounds for apprehending that any person by his action intends to provoke a breach of the peace and that such action will result in a breach of the peace it is his duty to prevent that action. It is also the general duty of the police to protect life and property.[3]

The concept of the internal security of a State implies a continuance of the state of law and order, wherein the authority of the State and its officers is recognized and obeyed. That security can never be endangered except by the actual or threatened commission of crime. Any action which does not contravene or threaten to contravene the law cannot itself

---

[1] *Wolpe & others* v. *O.C., S.A. Police, Johannesburg*, 1955 (2) S.A. 87.
[2] Ib. at 94.
[3] Halsbury's *Laws of England* (Hailsham ed.), vol. 25, para. 529.

threaten internal security of the State. Consequently, such action should need no police surveillance or investigation. The position created by the amendment of the Police Act of 1955, which defined the functions of the police force,[1] was, therefore, merely a restatement of what under the common law had always been a police function, namely, the duty to keep watch and ward against the actual or threatened commission of crimes whether directed at the security of the State or at private individuals. Preventive action by the police in relation to threatened crime is lawful only where there are reasonable grounds for believing that the conduct interfered with by the police in the exercise of their preventive function, is likely to result in an *imminent* or *reasonably proximate* offence.[2]

How has this concept of the police function of preserving the internal security of the Union received recognition in the latter's statute law?

Prior to 1955, the privacy of one's home against arbitrary intrusion by officers of the police was in general safeguarded by the necessity for obtaining a search-warrant from a judge, a magistrate, or a justice of the peace. Complaint on oath was a necessary formality and the officer applying for such a warrant had to satisfy the judicial officer concerned that there were reasonable grounds for suspecting that there was upon any person or any premises or in or upon any vehicle or any receptacle:

(*a*) stolen property or anything with respect to which any offence had been or was suspected on reasonable grounds to have been committed;

(*b*) anything in respect of which there were reasonable grounds for believing that it would afford evidence as to the commission of an offence;

(*c*) anything in respect of which there were reasonable grounds for believing that it was intended to be used for committing an offence.

The warrant to search was issued only in these three instances. It authorized any policeman to search any person found upon

---

[1] Act 15 of 1955 (the Police Amendment Act, 1955), sec. 3.
[2] *Thomas* v. *Sawkins*, [1935] 2 K.B. 249 at 255.

such premises and to seize the *thing* suspected of being upon him or the premises.[1]

It should be emphasized that the power of search mentioned above was a restricted one. Entry into premises and search were authorized solely in relation to a thing or object sought and only where that object was reasonably suspected of being *related* to the commission of an offence either because it was used for that purpose or because it might afford evidence of a suspected crime or because it was intended to be used for any crime. If there was no relationship reasonably suspected of existing between the object sought by means of the search-warrant and any crime either committed or threatened, the justification for authorizing a search was lacking.

The need to apply for a warrant was, however, relaxed in those cases where, owing to delay in obtaining it, the object of the search would be defeated, but here, too, relaxation was permissible only where there were *reasonable grounds for believing that delay would defeat that object* and where the reasonable belief was entertained by a police officer *of experience and responsibility* —a qualification which the legislature set at the rank of sergeant or above.[2]

This right to search still exists but the important safeguard mentioned in the preceding paragraph has now been removed.[3] The new Criminal Code permits *any* policeman of whatever rank to enter and search without warrant in the circumstances already mentioned. There is, of course, some precedent for this in what have always been recognized as conditions peculiar to South Africa, for example the right of search without warrant of a policeman holding a rank designated by the Minister,[4] where stock or produce as defined by the Stock Theft laws is concerned, or where any substance concerned in a contravention of the law relating to intoxicating liquor, habit-forming drugs, and, more recently, fire-arms, is affected.[5] In these

[1] Act 31 of 1917, as amended, sec. 49(1), now Act 56 of 1955, sec. 42.

[2] Act 31 of 1917, as amended, sec. 50(1).

[3] Act 56 of 1955, sec. 43—the Criminal Procedure Act, 1955 (called the 'Criminal Code').

[4] See Government Notice 431 of 1918 promulgated under Act 31 of 1917, sec. 51(1). *Union Gazette*, 28 March, 1918, p. 576—designating every European policeman.

[5] Act 31 of 1917, sec. 51, as amended by Act 46 of 1935, sec. 7.; Act 26 of 1923, secs. 6 and 7; Act 56 of 1955, sec. 46.

special cases public opinion has accepted the view that it is desirable that any European constable, irrespective of his rank, should have the power of entry, and the reasonableness of granting such a power, for example, where a constable on patrol in a remote country district is investigating the theft of stock, is readily accepted. But the exception only demonstrates the validity of the rule that private property should, for the purposes of search, be subject to intrusion without warrant only where reasonable grounds exist for believing that *something* relating to a crime committed or threatened is to be found there, and the legislature has in the past for many years required the opinion of an officer whose rank provides some assurance of responsibility to be taken on that point. Why it has now conferred on any constable of the force, no matter how inexperienced, the right to make a decision, which it previously regarded as safely reposed only in a policeman of the rank of sergeant or above, is not apparent. The history of police administration in the Union in latter years is not one to support such an extension of power.

But there is a situation more fraught with danger to the individual's right of privacy than the one mentioned. The hitherto-accepted principle that the right to search was given for the purpose of enabling the police to obtain an *object* which in some way was related to or connected with a crime already committed or still threatened has received a far-reaching extension in section 44 of the Criminal Code of 1955. That section reads as follows:

44. (1) If it appears to a judge of a superior court, a magistrate, or justice on complaint made on oath that there are reasonable grounds for believing—

(a) that the internal security of the Union or the maintenance of law and order is likely to be endangered by or in consequence of any meeting which is being or is about to be held in or upon any premises; or

(b) that an offence has been or is being or is likely to be committed or that preparations or arrangements for the commission of any offence are being or are likely to be made in or upon any premises,

he may issue a warrant directing a policeman named therein or all policemen to enter the said premises at any reasonable time for the purpose of carrying out such investigations and of taking such reasonable steps as such policeman or policemen may consider necessary for the preservation of the internal security of the Union or the maintenance of law and order or for the prevention of the commission of any offence, and for the purpose of searching such premises or any person in or upon such premises for anything which such policeman or policemen may have reasonable grounds for suspecting to be in or upon such premises or upon such person and as to which he or they may have reasonable grounds for believing that it will afford evidence as to the commission of any offence or that it is intended to be used for the purpose of committing any offence, and to seize any such thing, if found, and to take it before a magistrate.

(2) If any policeman believes on reasonable grounds that the delay in obtaining a warrant under sub-section (1) would defeat the objects of such a warrant, he may himself at all reasonable times, enter the premises concerned without warrant and there carry out such investigations and take such reasonable steps as he may consider necessary for the preservation of the internal security of the Union or the maintenance of law and order, or for the prevention of the commission of any offence, and if he has reasonable grounds for suspecting that there is in or upon the said premises or upon any person in or upon the said premises anything as to which there are reasonable grounds for believing that it will afford evidence as to the commission of any offence or that it is intended to be used for the purpose of committing any offence, he may without warrant search such premises or such person for any such thing and may seize such thing if found and take it before a magistrate.

(3) Whenever any policeman in the investigation of any offence or alleged offence has reasonable grounds for believing that there is upon any premises any person who is able to give evidence in relation to the commission of that offence he may without warrant enter the said premises for the purpose of interrogating the said person and for taking a statement from him.

(4) Any policeman may use such force as may be necessary to obtain entry to any premises which he is authorized to enter in terms of sub-section (1), (2) or (3) or to overcome any resistance offered against his entry thereto, and may, if necessary, for that purpose break open any door or window of such premises: Provided that no policeman shall act under this sub-section unless he has previously failed to obtain admission after having audibly demanded the same and notified the purpose for which he seeks to enter such premises: Provided further that nothing in this sub-section or sub-section (3) contained shall authorize a policeman to enter the

private dwelling of any person for the purpose referred to in sub-section (3), except with the consent of the occupier of that dwelling.

(5) If a woman is searched under any of the provisions of this section, the provisions of sub-section (3) of section thirty-six shall *mutatis mutandis* apply.

(6) Any person who wilfully obstructs, resists or hinders a police-man in the execution of any duty or the exercise of any power under this section, shall be guilty of an offence and liable on con-viction to a fine not exceeding one hundred pounds or to imprison-ment for a period not exceeding six months or to both such fine and such imprisonment.

It will be seen that the circumstances which may now give rise to the issue of a warrant authorizing entry into private premises are *not* qualified by those which were the distinguishing feature of entry and search in the Criminal Code of 1917.

Entry and search in relation to the internal security of the Union is not necessarily associated in section 44(1)(a) with a belief, held on reasonable grounds, that anything is to be found on the premises which will afford evidence of the com-mission of a crime or a threatened crime. Nor is it necessarily associated with a reasonable belief that a crime has been or is likely to be committed or that preparations are being made to commit one. If this were so, there would be no need for para-graph (a) of section 44(1) since the provisions of section 42 of the Criminal Code of 1956 and section 44(1)(b) would confer all necessary power to that end. What is contemplated in para-graph (a) of section 44(1) is, it seems, a reasonable belief that the internal security of the Union is likely to be endangered by or in consequence of a meeting, which is in all respects, a lawful and constitutional one! If, of course, it is not a lawful and constitutional one, the provisions of paragraph (b) of section 44(1) or section 42 are readily available to secure entry and search. If an offence is likely to be committed at the meeting or preparations are being set on foot to commit an offence, paragraph (b) gives adequate power to the police to deal with that situation.

Now to say that a meeting lawfully constituted and con-ducted endangers the internal security of the State, is to assert a contradiction in terms. The gathering is, *ex hypothesi*, a lawful one. Its proceedings, too. are lawful, since, if they were not, an offence would be committed or threatened or be in the course of preparation and the police could invoke the powers conferred by section 44(1)(b). The sole foundation for invoking paragraph (a) of that section in relation to the security of the State must therefore be one which, while conceding the lawful character of the meeting, its proceedings, and the intention of its promoters and audience, asserts that the mere holding of the meeting is likely to endanger the internal security of the State. That, however, it can only rightly be said to do if it is reasonably believed that persons *other than those lawfully holding and attending the meeting* are likely to be influenced to break the law as a result of that meeting or what lawfully occurs there. As we are assuming a meeting held and conducted in lawful circumstances, this can only happen if such *third* persons break the law in a way which can have no legally causal connexion with the meeting. In the result one arrives at the conclusion that the legislature has now authorized police intrusion into private premises, when no reasonable belief exists that any offence has been or is being, or is likely to be, committed by those present or by anyone else for whose acts those present at the meeting can be held legally responsible; further, that this is so when no reasonable belief exists that preparations for an offence are being, or are likely to be, made at the meeting. The right to intrude is given, it appears, solely because what is thought will be said or done at the meeting, albeit completely lawful in character, is likely to endanger the internal security of the Union or to have that consequence.

Put in plain terms, this is tantamount to subjecting completely lawful conduct carried out at a meeting in the privacy of a home or at any lawful gathering in a private place, for example a dinner party, to police intrusion and surveillance because of feared consequences which the persons taking part in the gathering do not desire, may indeed expressly disapprove, and for which they cannot be held legally responsible. The privacy of any meeting together of peaceful citizens is open to be disrupted by police presence because it is feared that the expressed thoughts of its members and guests, completely lawful in themselves, may give rise to breaches of the law by others.

Thus, advocacy, at a private meeting, of manhood suffrage for all races in the Union could, it seems conceivable, reasonably give rise in the present climate of political philosophy to grounds for fearing that the consequence of such a meeting would be likely later to be demands by others that would disrupt the internal security of the State. If this is a reasonable ground, as it might well be regarded, for obtaining police intervention in a meeting, no political creed which preached far-reaching but constitutional reform could be free from police surveillance and interference, no matter where expressed!

The impact of this obscure phrase in section 44(1)(a) — 'likely to endanger the internal security of the Union'—upon the individual's right to associate, and to discuss and criticize freely within the limits of the law, is profoundly disturbing. It needs no vivid imagination to visualize situations within the field of constitutional reform or within the field of religion which the prevailing trend of thought in this country would consider a basis for fearing for the future internal security of the State. Indeed, the view has already been expressed in Parliament that free association in urban areas of Europeans and Africans within the Church leads to the creation of 'nuisances' by Africans through the mere fact of their presence as black people passing through European residential areas. If any doubt is felt as to the reality of the danger to liberty latent in section 44(1)(a), a reading of the report of the debate on the subject in the House of Assembly will dispel that doubt.[1]

The root objection to paragraph (a) of section 44(1) is that it opens the doors of private homes and free and lawful gatherings of citizens to the intrusion of police officers on the mere belief that thoughts lawfully expressed there are likely to issue in action for reform which, however constitutional itself, is considered to be likely to have as a consequence (indeed, it may only be a remote consequence in point of time) unlawful action by *others*.

It will be said, of course, that the belief that a meeting or gathering will have this consequence must be a reasonable one, that a judicial officer must so regard it before authorizing any warrant, and that that is an adequate safeguard to the privacy

---

[1] *Hansard*, vol. 87 (1955), col. 1424 et seq.

of the home and the right of private association. This answer nowhere meets the fundamental criticism of this latently tyrannical power, which is: that conduct wholly lawful in itself is subjected to the risk and embarrassment of police surveillance, suspicion, and interference because of possible consequences for which the original actors cannot be held responsible in law. Surely in these circumstances the police function is a simple one—to prevent breaches of the law by those who threaten public order, and not to disrupt the privacy of a lawful proceeding.

Apart, however, from this basic objection, which applies even where judicial officers are authorized to issue warrants to enter and search, there is a further consideration raised by subsection (2) of section 44. That subsection authorizes a policeman *of any rank* to enter and search without a warrant in the same circumstances as would entitle him to obtain a warrant, provided, however, that he believes on reasonable grounds that the delay in procuring it would defeat its object.

Even if it be conceded that something might be said in support of the view that it was desirable to remove the minimum qualification of the rank of sergeant which applied before 1956 to a search by a member of the police force who believed on reasonable grounds that delay on procuring a warrant might defeat the object of the warrant, it must be remembered that the removal of this requirement by section 43 applied in the limited class of case there mentioned. The judgement there called for on the part of an ordinary constable related to action restricted in its scope, upon which there could be some hope, if not complete assurance, that a due discretion would be exercised. But the judgement and discretion which subsection (2) of section 44 expects from a constable relate to a question the nicety and vagueness of which might well baffle the intellectual powers of a judge, let alone someone whose entrance to the force is based on a limited educational qualification. Where then is the assurance to the individual that his home or right of privacy is adequately safeguarded against arbitrary executive intrusion? The penalty of a £50 fine and a liability to pay damages not exceeding £100 for malicious or unreasonable use of the power is unlikely in these circumstances to prove a weighty deterrent.[1] If there be added to this the consideration that the power is likely to be used in many instances when the less-privileged section of the community is pressing for reform, the risks of its arbitrary exercise are immeasurably increased.

It cannot too often be emphasized that entry and search without a warrant under paragraph (a) of subsection (1) of section 44, read with subsection (2) of that section, would not be to investigate a crime already committed, or to prevent one likely to be committed or one actually being prepared. All this is covered by the powers conferred by paragraph (b). The purpose of invoking paragraph (a) would be simply to allow the police to be present at a private meeting in order to listen or put a stop to discussion lawful in itself but deemed likely to endanger the internal security of the Union. The possibility of anyone's challenging any unlawful intrusion at the moment of entry is remote when regard is had to the penalties for 'hindering' a policeman in the exercise of any power conferred by the section.[2]

At the time of writing this, an amendment to section 26 of the Police Act of 1912[3] introduces an additional element into the offence of obstructing or hindering the police, namely, 'interfering'. It might well be that the intention of our lawmakers is to penalize any interference—even a verbal and indignant remonstration aimed at persuading the police to abandon an action already embarked upon. One does not know how courts will interpret this amendment should it become law, but some support for the possibility suggested can be found in the case of *Sykes* v. *Barraclough*,[4] where inflammatory speeches and advice given to certain miners were held to constitute 'interference with workmen' in contravention of the Coal Mines Regulation Act (1887) of England. The Minister during the debate on the Bill adopted the reasons for its introduction given by the Commissioner of Police, namely, that it was intended to deal with 'busybodies'.

Section 44(1) and (2) thus places it within the power of a police officer to compel the termination of a meeting both constitutional and legal, all in the cause of preserving the

---

[1] Act 56 of 1955, sec. 45.   [2] Ib., sec. 44(6).
[3] Police Act Amendment Act, No. 32 of 1957, sec. 26 *ter* (a).
[4] [1904] 2 K.B. 678.

THE POLICE FORCE

39

internal security of the Union. He alone is the judge of what is necessary to preserve that security. The powers conferred by this legislation make deep inroads into the liberties of the subject. They could be justified in the extreme circumstances of a State at war or on the verge of revolution. To confer them in peacetime creates a situation close to arbitrary executive control — a hall-mark of the police state. If mere lawful advocacy of constitutional reform is capable of being regarded as likely to have consequences dangerous to the internal security of the State, if this is something which could give rise to police investigation and surveillance in a private meeting, if this is to afford ground for the presence of the police, free and lawful discussion becomes suspect as contrary to the interests of the State, legitimate and constitutional reform acquires disrepute, and the rights of association and criticism are stifled. Reform through argument and persuasion, however constitutional, is subjected to the uncomfortable notice of the police, and democratic processes will die.

So much then for the legislature's inroads on the liberty of the subject through the extension of these wide powers to the police. What, however, of the manner of administration of such other powers as have admittedly reasonably been granted to the police? And what of the change in character and outlook of the force itself, induced by a new, subtle emphasis and interpretation placed on the idea of the internal security of the State?

It is true that the illegal use of power reasonably granted to the police is no argument with which to support a submission that the freedom of the subject has been curtailed with the approval of the State. Excess in the use of lawful power is not countenanced by the laws of the Union, and a subject injured in his rights by any such excess has his civil remedy. Theoretically, the State will itself punish any such excess if it involves a contravention of the criminal law. But executive action which is arbitrary and in excess of the law nevertheless closely touches the liberty of the subject if it goes undetected and unpunished. This it might do in circumstances where the injured persons have a status something less than that of citizens, are uneducated, ignorant, and treated by society as a subject race. If these conditions prevail in society, the liberty of the subject is as much lost as it would be if the legislature had removed it by statutory provision.

Can it be said that the exercise or administration of lawful and necessary power conferred on the police has in this country exhibited these characteristics? Bona fide and erroneous excess of power is a feature of any form of administration dependent upon human agency. But that case apart, it cannot be disputed that there is a wide and increasing field of regimentation in the life of the African peoples in which excess of lawful power and arbitrary action by the police is inherently possible. That it does occur is certain. Only a small number of these cases come to light. That is not surprising, for, in the innumerable arrests and searches which are a common feature of African urban life, few Africans have the education, means, or time to challenge excess, whether it occur bona fide or mala fide. The power of the police has been elevated to such a degree and is so formidable that it would require qualities of moral courage and pertinancity that the average European, let alone the illiterate African, cannot afford to display.

That this *administrative* danger to the freedom of the subject exists in the powers of the police is demonstrated by what occurred in *Wolpe's* case.[1] There the entry by the police into a private meeting was sought to be justified in court proceedings on the ground, *inter alia*, that the police believed that certain persons would attend the meeting who had already been prohibited from attending that class of meeting. The Court held that this was no justification for the entry and that the police could and should have done their duty by watching for any such persons *outside* the premises concerned. It is noteworthy that high-ranking police officers sought to justify this invasion of the individual's privacy—an excess of power which the Court held was not justified. In that case the persons affected were educated and aware of their rights. If this was the attitude of men of experience in the force, what are the risks of invasion in the numerous petty cases that affect the uneducated public?

To take another example. Recently the police force was heavily engaged in Johannesburg in harrying all who took part

---

[1] *Wolpe & another*, see footnote 1, p. 29.

in the bus boycott. Africans who walked to their employment
were stopped at check points along the road into the city, and
the full weight of the laws which affect their lives was brought
to bear on them. Passes were called for. Every possible contravention of the laws of which they might be guilty was raised
as a pretext for making the boycott unpleasant and difficult
for those who participated. The licensing laws for vehicles, the
motor-vehicle transportation laws—all were called in aid by
the police. Europeans who assisted by transporting workmen
to their employment were stopped repeatedly on the pretext
of police investigation of possible contravention of the motor
laws and the Road Transportation Act.

It is therefore hardly to be doubted that the probabilities
favour the existence of many instances never brought to light,
where through ignorance and the other factors mentioned
administrative excess of police power occurs and goes unchal-
lenged. But if Parliament by its legislation encourages contempt
for the individual's liberty, the pattern for administrative
excess is already set. Is it then to be wondered at if it occurs?

There is, however, another and a sinister aspect of the
administrative excess of police power, which has come into
prominence lately. It is the new emphasis placed administratively, and endorsed legislatively,[1] on the concept of the
internal security of the Union.

Of the emphasis placed on this idea by the legislature we
have already spoken. The administrative emphasis lies, among
other things, in the employment of the police in the new role
of 'political police'. We say 'political police' advisedly, because,
in the discharge of the function of preserving the internal
security of the Union, the relationship of crime committed or
reasonably apprehended with the internal security has been
lost sight of to such an extent that innocent, lawful, and constitutional conduct by reputable citizens calls forth the attentions of the Special Branch of the police. Today, police
attention is closely directed to all activities where reform
affecting the non-European section of the community is concerned. The Native Laws Amendment Act of 1957[2] gives
legislative expression, ostensibly in the cause of apartheid, to

---

[1] Act 15 of 1955, sec. 3; Act 56 of 1955, sec. 44.
[2] Act 36 of 1957. See sec. 29.

an administrative practice of the security police which, fundamentally, is based on regarding all forms of communication
between European and non-European as potentially likely to
endanger the internal security of the Union. That attitude of
the Special Branch manifests itself in the attendance of its
officers at meetings, lawful and constitutional, where citizens
of standing have met to utter their protest and petition against
certain laws. By no stretch of imagination could these gatherings
be linked with crime or any threat to the internal security of
the realm. Yet the attendance of individuals, often ascertained
by noting the registered numbers of their motor vehicles, is
observed and noted in the archives of the Security Branch. Of
such a piece, too, are the visits of members of that Branch to
private homes, and their inquiries, and the attentions of police
photographers flashing their flashlights as reminders to those
who constitutionally meet or lawfully march in procession,
and who in reasonable debate discuss and criticize the laws of
the State, that even this freedom is purchased at the cost of
embarrassing police attention and suspicion.

The discharge of a professional duty as an attorney and
officer of the court recently received the attention of a Special
Branch photographer, who photographed the attorney concerned as he left the court precincts with his clients. An apology
and explanation of mistaken identity followed, but, as the
attorney said in his protest to the magistrate, the significance
of the police action would be lost on no one.[1]

It is apparent from all this that there is much that is dis-
tressing and ominous in the method of administering this
function of preserving the internal security of the Union. The
new concept of the police function tends to clothe the police
force with the character of the political police of authoritarian
rule. The manner in which it has been compelled to administer
its function of preserving the internal security of the Union has
impressed an instrument once designed to serve the interests
of justice and to elevate the rule of law, with the character of
a political instrument serving the private interests of governmental power.

[1] *Sunday Times*, Johannesburg, 26 May 1957.

CHAPTER IV

Racial Discrimination: Is it fundamental in South African Law?

The object of this chapter is not to discuss whether there are laws discriminating against non-Europeans on the Statute Book of the Union. All the world knows that there are such laws. Nor is it to prove that in every sphere of life, and in the basic principles of the administration of justice, there is a complete theoretical differentiation on the grounds of race and colour. This is demonstrably not the case. What we are seeking to discover is the extent to which discrimination on racial lines exists in South African law, and whether in any but a rhetorical sense this can be said to be 'fundamental'.

We begin with Parliament, and here we must start with the very document to which Parliament owes its existence—the South Africa Act of 1909. That Act, in sections 26 and 44, lays down that every member of Parliament must be 'a British subject of *European descent*'. The political structure of the Union, the composition of the body which makes the laws, thus has the colour bar at its heart. By the same Act the pre-Union franchise laws of the four colonies were preserved, which meant a complete colour bar as regards voting rights in the Transvaal and the Orange Free State. Subsequent legislation (see Chapter XI for the details) dealt with the small number of non-European voters in the Cape and the infinitesimal number in Natal, so that today no non-European voter may be placed on the general electoral roll, and the representation of non-Europeans in Parliament is confined to the election of a fixed and small number of Europeans, chosen by voters on separate racial rolls, African and 'Cape Coloured', which latter term includes qualified Indian voters in the Cape Province. At the very heart of the legislative system, therefore, there is an almost complete exclusion of non-Europeans, whose representation is small, fixed in numbers and precarious.

43

What of the Executive? By law or convention, non-Europeans are excluded from the office of Governor-General, from the Cabinet, and from all higher posts in the public service. Much of this exclusion is conventional, though conventions are often harder to change than statutes are, but exclusion from the Cabinet is a matter of law, for any Minister who does not obtain a seat in one of the two Houses of Parliament within three months of appointment forfeits his office,[1] and no non-European may become a member of either House of Parliament.

This principle of exclusion goes very far down. Thus no African has ever been appointed a Native commissioner (magistrate) or assistant Native commissioner (assistant magistrate), even in a purely African area. One African with very high legal qualifications was a few years ago considered for appointment as assistant Native commissioner in the Transkeian Territories, but it was felt to be more judicious not to put him in a position where European attorneys would have to address him as 'your Worship'. To go still lower down the scale, General Smuts, as Minister of Defence, issued an order during the Second World War that where a mixed body of South African soldiers was isolated without a commissioned officer,[2] the highest-ranking European should take command of the party even though a higher-ranking non-European should be present; for example a European private would take precedence over an African sergeant. As far as possible no non-European is ever put by the State in authority over any European: if such a situation arises it is regarded as anomalous and most undesirable, requiring to be terminated as speedily as possible.

This is very fundamental in the social and administrative structure of present-day South Africa, though, to be sure, most of it is the result of rigid convention rather than of law.

What of the Judiciary? No formal barrier keeps non-Europeans from the Bar or the Side Bar, and there are a few non-European advocates and attorneys. The Minister of Justice recently (1957) made a speech in which he said that he might have to introduce legislation to restrict their activities in courts. None has ever been made a Q.C., and, naturally enough

---

[1] South Africa Act, sec. 14.

[2] No non-European has ever held a commission in the South African Defence Force.

in these circumstances, none has been elevated to the bench. This, too, is a matter of convention, not of law. No non-European may sit on a jury, but it is competent for a judge to summon one or two non-Europeans to assist him as assessors.[1]

The judges of the South African Supreme Court have in the past won an enviable reputation for integrity and impartiality, and the non-Europeans have looked with great confidence to the judicial bench (even though they are excluded from it) for the protection of their interests. But South African judges are, in general, like their brethren in the United Kingdom, bound by the strict wording of Acts of Parliament. When Acts direct them to differentiate between Europeans and non-Europeans, they must, of course, do so to the extent clearly indicated by the Act, and an increasing number of Acts do so direct them. Let us look at some examples.

One of these statutes is the Population Registration Act, by which every South African must be registered as a white person, a coloured person, or a Native, and every coloured person or Native also classified according to the ethnic or other sub-group to which he belongs.[2] The population register is supposed to record (though so far desire has outrun performance) the marital status and address of every citizen and to be used for purposes of the voters' roll,[3] and it would appear that race distinction is thereby made fundamental in the Union.

Moreover, it is impossible to escape from one's classification, and not easy for one's descendants to do so. There is no provision in the Population Registration Act for racial promotion or demotion. Nature may of course take a hand, but so vital an institution as marriage is brought into this fundamental differentiation. By the Prohibition of Mixed Marriages Act (No. 55 of 1949) all marriages between Europeans and non-Europeans are prohibited. Subject to certain not very numerous exceptions,[4] all such marriages are void, and any marriage officer knowingly performing a marriage of this kind is liable to a fine.[5] The Immorality Amendment Act (No. 21 of 1950) prohibits all illicit carnal intercourse, even with consent,

---

[1] Act 56 of 1955, secs. 114 and 119.
[2] Act 30 of 1950, sec. 5.
[3] This appears to follow from ib., sec. 7(1)(f).
[4] Act 55 of 1949, sec. 1(1).   [5] Ib., sec. 2.

between a European and a non-European. The principle had already been laid down by Act No. 5 of 1927 with regard to illicit carnal intercourse between Europeans and Africans: the amending Act extended the prohibition to all non-Europeans.

If in spite of the law intercourse takes place and if a child is born, its classification will, of course, be 'coloured'. The only possibility of its being registered as 'white' will be in the case of a white woman having an illegitimate child by a non-European man, when (a) the authorities are unaware that the father is non-European, and (b) the child is European in appearance.

In course of time the operation of the population register, if it is complete—it is far from complete at present—may result in a small number of persons with fair hair, blue eyes, and fresh complexions being classified as 'coloured', and a small number of dark-haired, brown-eyed, sallow persons being classified as 'white'. Such anomalies exist at present, but in the past the blue-eyed blonde has, as in the United States, been able by moving from his neighbourhood to 'pass' and be recognized as a white man: this, if the population register is complete and efficiently administered, should henceforth be all but impossible. To escape from this hereditary classification may, as indicated earlier in Chapter II, be possible by a direct appeal (not by 'passing'), but this is uncertain.

The study of the Group Areas Act in Chapter II has shown clearly how this very fundamental classification is the basis which determines where a man may live, and where he may carry on his business. This and other laws have been carried very far. For example, an African advocate has been refused permission to have chambers with the other advocates in Johannesburg.[1] An Indian advocate in Natal has now been assigned a special robing-room in the Supreme Court in Durban. Separate witness-boxes for white and black have been installed also. Curiously, the Indian advocate enters the court by the same door as his colleagues, and once in court sits at the Bar with them.

Separate amenities based on racial differentiation are a matter partly of law, partly of convention. In one way or

[1] In Salisbury, Southern Rhodesia, a similar case was decided, though not without difficulty in the opposite sense.

another they are the norm of life in the Union. The Factories Acts require separate toilets and rest-rooms for Europeans and non-Europeans. Custom produces the same result in blocks of offices and flats. The South African Railways provide separate 'reserved' first- and second-class accommodation for non-Europeans—no European today travels third class—and separate waiting-rooms are also provided. Recently the influence of the Union Department of Transport has been used to push for the separation of passengers on buses and trams in the few cities where it does not already exist. But there is no need to go into further detail. The separation of amenities is very general, and is one of the first aspects of South African life to strike any visitor from overseas.

It might be expected that this separation would be based on the famous formula 'separate but equal', and this is what the South African courts laid down as recently as in the case of *Rex* v. *Lusu* (1953)[1]—a clear indication that up to that date the courts held to the doctrine of equality, at least, if not to the doctrine of integration, in the absence of legislation to the contrary. But by the Reservation of Separate Amenities Act (No. 49 of 1953) it is laid down that the separate amenities need not be 'substantially similar to or of the same character, standard, extent or quality' as 'those set aside for the other race'.[2]

Both the Statute Book and the administrative practice of the Union teem with instances of separation in amenities based on racial grounds. The courts are now prevented, by the express terms of Act 49 of 1953, from insisting that these separate amenities shall be equal amenities.

Another sphere in which racial differentiation appears to be fundamental is that of social welfare, and in particular of social pensions or grants. Thus, as regards old-age pensions, for Europeans the maximum pension is £114 per annum (with a means-plus-pension limitation of £162 per annum); for Coloured persons £49 10s. per annum (with a means-plus-pension limitation of £81); for Indians £43 10s. per annum (with a means-plus-pension limitation of £66); for Africans living in large cities £12 per annum (with a means-plus-pension limitation of £36); for Africans living in smaller cities

---

[1] 1953 (2) S.A. 484.   [2] Act 49 of 1953, sec. 3(*b*).

£9 per annum (with a means-plus-pension limitation of £27);
for Africans living in rural areas and reserves £6 per annum
(with a means-plus-pension limitation of £18).

Blind pensions are at similar rates with the difference that
only half the earnings of a blind person may be taken into
account in assessing his means.

Disability pensions are at the same rate as old-age pensions
with similar limitations, except in the case of Africans, where
the amount of the grant is such as the Secretary for Native
Affairs deems reasonable and sufficient for the applicant's
maintenance, not exceeding £12 per annum, with a means test
of £24.

Military pensions are scaled down in a similar manner.

Family allowances and children's maintenance grants do not
extend to all non-European groups. Unemployment benefits are
not paid to Africans. Workmen's compensation benefits and
silicosis benefits are at differential and diminishing rates for
Europeans, non-Europeans other than Africans, and Africans.

Thus, through the whole field of benefits provided in the
Welfare State the fundamental distinction between Europeans
and non-Europeans is steadily maintained.

The assumption underlying these differential rates is that
the standard of living of each of the non-European groups
differs from that of the others, and all from that of the Europeans. In broad terms this is true, though the difference in
rates is probably disproportionate (especially in the case of
Africans) to the difference in average standard of living. But
what of the considerable number of Africans whose standard of
living is as high as the average Indian standard, or of those
Indians whose standard of living is as high as the average
European standard? And if it be objected that to give higher
benefits to these is to give most help to the least needy cases, on
what basis can we justify the higher benefits given to Europeans?
However we argue, we come back to the point that the main
criterion is race and (except for internal subdivisions within the
African group based on place of residence) race alone.

Thus, so far as statute law goes, race differentiation is fundamental in South African life in so wide a variety of matters as
to touch most of the material issues of daily life. But what of
those situations which are not covered by statute? Is

race differentiation applicable to them as a matter of principle?

The practice of administration is to assume this. Few public servants would depart from it, even in minor matters, and anyone who did would be in danger of being censured by his Department.

There remain the courts. It would probably be safe to say that up to the present the superior courts of the Union still regard the absence of discrimination as the rule in the limited area where statutory provisions to the contrary do not operate. Indeed, in the debate in the House of Assembly on the Reservation of Separate Amenities Bill, which followed on the Appellate Division's decision in the case of *Rex* v. *Lusu*, instances were quoted where Ministers had in public speeches attacked the Judges of Appeal for a supposed 'liberal bias'.[1] Nationalist members, on the other hand, quoted earlier judgments of the Appellate Division of the Supreme Court which appeared to indicate a conditional acceptance of a fundamental principle of differentiation.[2]

It is obvious that this is a most difficult as well as a most delicate point to establish. The existence of judicial prepossessions, if such exist, and their nature, is a subject which may well await a new book. Such a study can hardly be dealt with adequately as a footnote, so to speak, to a study of civil liberties. The kind of issues that arise are illustrated in the case of *Radebe* v. *Hough*, 1949 (1) S.A. 380 (A.D.) at 384–5. In this case a trial judge, in assessing the damages to be awarded to an African for physicial pain and suffering, said,

I am of opinion that in awarding damages for pain and suffering one must take into consideration the standing of the person injured. For instance, in the case of a native, as is the plaintiff, who is earning the sum of £2 per week, I should most certainly not award the same amount for pain and suffering as I would for the same pain and suffering of a person who had more culture, and for instance I would award a larger sum for damages in the case of an injury to a European woman than I would for a native male, and so too in the present case, if it had been a European of some standing I would have awarded greater damage than I now propose to do.

[1] e.g. House of Assembly *Hansard*, vol. 82, col. 2026.
[2] Ib., col. 2050.

In commenting upon this reasoning in the ensuing appeal to the Appellate Division, Hoexter, A.J.A., as he then was, said,

> It is the physical and mental make up of the person injured which must be considered in assessing his pain and suffering, and that make up cannot be determined by reference to his social or cultural or financial status. Most decidedly it cannot be determined by reference to his race. . . . But in my opinion the fact that the appellant is a native, earning only £2 a week, is not evidence that he is insensitive to pain.

In the same case, Hoexter, A.J.A., at 386, referred to two cases: *Jojo* v. *William Bain Co., Ltd.*, 1941 S.R. 72, and *Mkize* v. *The South British Insurance Co., Ltd.*, 1948 (4) S.A. 33 at 36, in the following terms:

> In each of the above cases the Court appears to have taken into consideration the fact that the injured person was a native of very small means for whom money would have a very high value. In my opinion that fact should have been excluded from consideration.

In the light of this revealing case we may venture to put some of the questions which future research workers should face. Do the magistrates' courts assume that, in the absence of specific legislation to the contrary, colour discrimination is not part of South African law? Does the Supreme Court also assume this? To what extent are our courts, superior or inferior, influenced by the changing climate of public opinion? Are the variations in sentences passed in respect of the same crime (for example, rape) influenced directly by the colour of the accused or of the victim, or only by considerations not directly connected with colour?

To these questions it is impossible to give decided answers without careful and extensive research in a field outside the main scope of this study. We can only say that if such research led to the conclusion that colour discrimination was coming to be recognized as a fundamental assumption of South African law, then the last door of hope would be closed to non-Europeans in South Africa who have up to the present day looked with confidence to the courts, and especially to the Supreme Court, to protect them against any executive action which is not based upon specific statutory authority.

CHAPTER V

Freedom of Person in relation to
movement

The right to come and go freely within one's own country is so common a feature of countries where the British parliamentary tradition prevails that few white people in the Union pause to inquire to what extent that right is honoured in the laws of their own country. If reminded that banishment, without judicial decree, to certain areas of the Union exists, that restraints based on race operate in other cases to prevent whole classes of subjects from entering urban areas without permission from authority, many will dismiss these as exceptions which are necessary in the interests of orderly government. The exceptions however are becoming the rule.

The necessity for restraints on freedom of movement in a community recently subjected to conquest is indisputable where the conquering power is still engaged in establishing its authority. Ultimately, however, where Western notions of government prevail, the aim in such a case has been to bring about a progressive relaxation of restraints, and to enlarge the area of freedom.

Does the need for restriction of movement, assuming it to exist as a genuine political need in the Union, defer to any similar notion—the progressive relaxation of restrictions? The weight of present-day restrictions, admittedly, falls on the non-European peoples. In general they have long since submitted to the constitution, and loyally respected its laws and the power of lawfully constituted government. Such challenge to lawful authority as can be said to exist through pan-Africanism and communism derives much of its support from the very existence of these restrictions.

To inquire a little further whether the trend of legislation is leading in the direction of less restriction on freedom of movement, let us examine the position of the Indian population. The laws which restrict the free movement of Indians inter-provincially have their origin in the immigration laws of the pre-Union colonies and the republics of the Transvaal and the Orange Free State. As separate political entities these states were then entitled to regulate and prohibit entry into their respective territories. On the merger involved in Union, the subjects of each state became the subjects of the Union, and one would suppose all would have been accorded the right to move freely within the new State of which they had become subjects. The retention of those previous restrictions on Indians can only be justified on the same grounds as previously controlled their movement in South Africa by means of immigration laws which in the final assessment were based on distinctions of race. It is astonishing after forty-seven years of Union to see members of the population now indigenous to the country for several generations treated within their own land as immigrants whose movements into provinces where they are not domiciled is subjected to governmental control.

Restriction upon the freedom of movement of the African population has its origins in the protective measures taken by an early European frontier society to ensure the establishment of law and order and the continued existence of that society among peoples still in a state of barbarism. As the Europeans' order became more firmly established, restriction on movement took on a different character until, with the industrialization and growth of the urban centres, measures are now designed to keep the African in the Reserves and on the farms and away from the urban centres of European habitation, save to the extent that he is required as a servant or employee in these areas. The pattern of segregating the African away from the urban area and of regarding the latter as the white man's preserve is now imprinted on the social structure of the country by legislation such as the Natives (Urban Areas) Consolidation Act of 1945 and the Group Areas Act of 1950.

It must be conceded that justification can be found for controlling the movement of a rural and still backward people attracted by the higher cash wages of the urban centres. Problems of housing, health, the suppression of crime, call for some control, but the essence of all restrictions on the inward

movement of the African into the towns is that, even where
he is allowed to pass through the cordon, it is no longer on the
basis of his having the right to acquire a permanent domicile
in his place of employment but solely on the temporary footing
that he returns to the Reserve when his service has ended. Thus
the African subjects of the South African State are within their
own country confined, in a measure, within the separate
domiciliary areas authority has decreed for them. Departure
from these on a temporary basis requires the consent of
authority in the case of movement to the towns or from one
town to another. Permanent departure in order to take up a
fresh domicile elsewhere in other Reserves is not a simple
operation—official sanction to live in the new domicile is necessary. Permanent departure to live in the towns is not now
possible and the departure of an African who has acquired in
the past a domicile in a town to another area temporarily may
result in grave difficulties being placed in the way of his return
to the town of his domicile. In general the African requires some
form of authority or permission for any journey of consequence
within the Union. The law of the land regards him as having
true freedom of movement only within the circumscribed limits
of his own immediate domicile.

As for the European subject, he may in general travel any-
where without restriction save that he may not enter an
African Reserve, township, or location without permission.

So far we have mentioned the broad trend of the law in
relation to freedom of movement of the various races within
their own country. Apart from the general trend of restriction,
there exist special laws which confer on officials, without the
intervention of judicial decree, power to confine subjects to
certain areas either by requiring them not to leave the area
they reside in or by banishing them to areas other than their
homes. Reference to these will be made later in this chapter.
At the moment, we are concerned to present the fact that
despite a great movement in the past forty-seven years of
Union away from the needs of a frontier society, despite the
growth of education among non-Europeans and their incor-
poration into the economic structure of the country, despite
their presence in the towns as town-dwellers having all the
needs of town-dwellers, there has been no corresponding and

proportionate lessening of restriction upon their everyday life. What our forefathers deemed necessary in this way to protect their existence as a frontier society founded on conquest, we have in great measure preserved. We have gone further and added restrictions which have no place in a country where notions of freedom have any strength. And the reason? It is not easy to avoid the conclusion that in this respect society in South Africa is back where it was in the frontier days.

What follows is intended to show some of the inroads made into the personal freedom of the subject in this field, the pronounced increase in the tempo of encroachment since 1948 until today, where the position has been reached that for four-fifths of the population every journey taken from home is effected with the risk of coming into conflict with one or other of the regulations or laws which govern the movement of the non-European peoples. In other special instances, personal freedom in this field is subject to the unfettered discretion of some Minister or his delegate, who can by arbitrary order of confinement, without trial of any sort, without notice in some cases, and on information which he is not obliged fully to disclose, confine a person's liberty of movement to a specified area, prohibit him from attending gatherings, and banish him to another area or refuse him a passport to depart from the Union. All these pains and penalties which can be laid on the subject, white or black, do not arise necessarily because he has contravened the law of the land. They may and frequently do follow where no crime has been committed. There is no law that the subject should not speak in criticism of the government or advocate the repeal of laws honestly believed to be unjust. There was no law that he should not meet with or associate with men of different colour, even in the act of worship. But these things, even where they do not contravene the law, can be regarded as political offences upon which the whole baneful system of extrajudicial punishment can be brought to bear.

We proceed now to discuss the subject in more detail under the following two headings:

(a) general restrictions on freedom of movement forming the fabric of the laws controlling the non-European people;

(*b*) specific restrictions enforced administratively by way of preventive measure or penalty for political thought or action.

In the first category falls that body of laws and regulations which, as already stated, treats the Indian domiciled in one province as virtually an immigrant when he travels to another, and which under the name 'pass laws' treats the African's movements as soon as he leaves the reserves or his domicile as calling for special control.

(*a*) *General restrictions on freedom of movement forming the fabric of the laws controlling the African people*

The general contents of the so-called 'pass laws' have been summarized in many previous publications. All these references have become, from a formal and legal point of view, out of date since the passing of the Natives (Abolition of Passes and Co-ordination of Documents) Act, No. 67 of 1952. This Act abolishes a number of specific passes and replaces them with 'reference books', which are ultimately to be carried by all Africans over the age of 16 years, and in the meantime by Africans of such classes and resident in such areas as may be defined in notices issued by the Minister of Native Affairs in the *Government Gazette*.[1] The benefits of this change are vitiated by the following factors:

(1) The reference book is so far a glorified pass that failure to produce it to an 'authorised officer'[2] on demand involves the holder in a penalty of a fine not exceeding £10 or imprisonment not exceeding one month.[3]

(2) The reference book in some ways extends the pass system, since a variant of it has to be carried by persons hitherto exempted from the pass laws and may have to be carried by women.

(3) The curfew laws remain in force and special passes therefore have to be carried by Africans abroad during the hours of curfew.

---

[1] Act 67 of 1952, sec. 2, as amended by Act 79 of 1957, sec. 11. By the end of February 1956, reference books had been issued to 2,231,600 African men (Senate *Hansard*, col. 3877).

[2] A term which includes any policeman.

[3] Act 67 of 1952, sec. 15, as amended by Act 79 of 1957, sec. 24.

(4) The reference book is in no way a substitute for the many documents required under the Urban Areas Laws by Africans moving to the urban areas to look for employment, seeking for employment within the urban areas, and remaining in employment within them.

Let us take these points seriatim.

With reference to the first point—the liability to arrest if a reference book cannot be produced on demand—it may be mentioned that in 1953, the year after the passing of the Natives (Abolition of Passes and Co-ordination of Documents) Act, Africans to the number of 110,427 were convicted for offences against curfew regulations or regulations for registration and production of documents, and 43,951 for offences against the pass laws;[1] and in 1954, the largest proportion of the one million and a half prosecutions—27·8 per cent—was for 'offences against the pass laws, curfew regulations, regulations for the registration of Africans, Master and Servant Laws, laws relating to African taxation and other laws relating specifically to the control of Africans'.[2] It seems to be a case of 'new reference book is but old pass writ large'.

Coming to the second point—the extension of the reference-book system to persons hitherto not subject to the pass laws—it must be noted that the term 'Native male' is not used and that the term 'Native' is so defined as not to exclude women. Reference books for women were introduced in 1955 and were first issued in Winburg in the central Orange Free State in March 1956. Despite protests—which included in at least one instance the collection and burning of books—the government persists in the policy of extending the system to women, mainly in smaller towns. An official Native Affairs Department statement published in *The Star* on 15 August 1956 showed that up to that date 23,000 reference books had been issued to women.

There has been, and still is, considerable confusion as to the position under the new system of Africans previously exempted from the pass laws. Holders of letters of exemption and exemption certificates retain them but are issued in addition with reference books with green covers instead of the normal

---

[1] *A Survey of Race Relations in South Africa*, 1953–4 (South African Institute of Race Relations), p. 150.
[2] *A Survey of Race Relations in South Africa*, 1955–6 (S.A.I.R.R.), p. 232.

4

brown. They are subject to influx control and, unless the Native commissioner makes a suitable endorsement in the book, also to curfew regulations. Up to the time of writing, it has been impossible to secure from the Native Affairs Department a clear statement about the exact position of all exempted Africans, and they themselves are left in doubt.

That the new system still leaves the way open for harsh and oppressive action will appear from the following cases. *The Star* on 27 July 1956 told of an African employed as a gardener in Johannesburg who lives at Alexandra Township. When returning home one evening he was 'picked up' by the police. He was able to show that his reference book was in order and poll-tax paid; but he had no permit to live in Alexandra Township. He was unaware that such a permit is required, but ignorance is no excuse.

After being detained in the cells overnight, he was next morning sentenced to a fine of £3 or one month's imprisonment. Although he could have paid the fine from his savings, he did not carry that amount with him for fear of pickpockets, and he was not permitted to telephone his employer. He was, thus, sent to gaol.

There is a scheme whereby short-term African prisoners, if they volunteer to do so, are sent to serve their sentences on farms, the farmer paying ninepence a day for their services. This man alleged that he did not volunteer. Nevertheless, after two days in goal, during which, he said, he was heavily beaten by an African warder, he was sent to a farm near Heidelberg. As is the usual practice, his clothes were removed on arrival, and he was given a sack to wear with holes cut for his head and arms. Somehow or other his uncle managed to trace him and paid his fine. He returned to Johannesburg an embittered man.

Then there was the case of Mr. Simon Selane (eventually published in *The Star* of 30 July 1956), who was born in Pretoria and lived there all his life. He was thus fully entitled to remain. Through some Departmental error, however, his birthplace was stated in his reference book to be Duivelskloof. When he went, one day in February 1956, to register for a new job, his right to be in Pretoria was questioned and he was sent, on his bicycle, to the Native commissioner's office. He chose work on a farm as an alternative to prosecution. His bicycle was taken away and he was not permitted to get into touch with his relatives nor to fetch his clothes and blankets. That same day he was sent, with others, to a farm at Bethal to work for the stipulated wage of £3 per month plus food and accommodation. For months, despite repeated inquiries, his relatives heard nothing of him. When he eventually returned, he said that he had been repeatedly thrashed on the farm, so much so that he had spent a month in hospital, and that at the end of his contract he was driven to Bethal station and was paid only 3s. 6d. He walked to Witbank, many miles away, and there sold his jacket to raise money for the train-fare to Pretoria.

The Institute of Race Relations took up this case with the Department of Native Affairs, but received no explanation. Later, however, the Department issued a press statement (for example, *The Star*, 31 July 1956). An official of the labour bureau had visited the farm concerned and the hospital, it was said. It was untrue that Selane had been thrashed: he had been detained in hospital because of a knee condition caused by disease. Conditions on the farm were satisfactory and other workers had no complaints. The reason why Selane received only 3s. 6d. was that he had bought tobacco, matches, an overall, a pair of shoes, and an overcoat from the farmer. Selane's bicycle was returned to him. This statement did not explain why Mr. Selane, a bewildered, illiterate man, had not in the first place been permitted to prove his place of birth, nor to fetch his clothes, nor to communicate with his relatives.

There was the case, too (*Rand Daily Mail*, 18 August 1956), of a certified African mental patient awaiting admission to a mental hospital. Because of his condition he was unable to supply the information required for the issue of a reference book, but he carried a letter explaining the position. Yet he was arrested and sent to work on a farm near Springs. It took welfare workers three weeks to trace him; and the social worker who went to the farm to fetch him said that the labourers' compound there was filthy, the sacking used for matresses was infested with lice and bugs, and the chief diet was potatoes.

It is by no means suggested that all those debarred from the towns are sent to farms where they are ill-treated, but quite obviously under this system of influx control, mainly because of the very large numbers involved, Africans are treated as cyphers rather than as human beings, and increased supervision is required of conditions on the farms.

Considerable ill-feeling was caused when Cyprian Bhekuzulu, the Paramount Chief of the Zulus, and nine other members of the Zulu royal family were arrested in Durban during September 1956 for being out without passes, and were required to pay spot fines as an alternative to detention in gaol. The following month the Paramount Chief's aunt was arrested for a similar reason in Johannesburg when she had to spend the night in the cells. In both cases officials subsequently apologized, and the fines were returned.

During May 1956, two judges of the Supreme Court, Pretoria, concurred in upholding an appeal brought on behalf of Mr. Andries Mahlangu, who had been convicted of entering the Union, or accepting employment, or continuing in employment, without the authority of the Secretary for Native Affairs. Mr. Mahlangu originally came from Nyasaland, but had lived in Standerton since 1942, and had been in employment there up to the time that the case was instituted against him. He had paid his taxes regularly, had married a Standerton girl, and had occupied a house hired from the municipality. The location superintendent's evidence was that he had access to documents concerning Africans in the location, and according to these Mahlangu did not possess the necessary exemption or endorsement in his reference book. The judge ruled that the magistrate had erred in finding that there was a case to meet, since the evidence was quite inadequate. The Judge-President commented: 'This is so petty—so vindictive—so persecutory. ... Why not let the man stay? ... My sympathies are with the accused.' He suggested that the Attorney-General should consult with the Native Affairs Department with a view to making exceptions in special cases, in which the interpretation of the law should be benign.

The curfew regulations cause a very large number of arrests annually, but the most complicated and perhaps the most irksome of the regulations controlling freedom of movement are those governing the influx of Africans into urban areas and their employment in such areas. These regulations are considered at length, along with other labour legislation, in

Chapter VII (Economic Freedom), and the reader is referred
to the details given there. One instance may, however, be
given at this stage as showing the general insecurity of Africans
in urban areas. We take the example of section 27 of Act 54 of
1952 inserting a new section 10 into the Natives (Urban Areas)
Consolidation Act, No. 25 of 1945. This is the provision which
prohibits any African from 'remaining' in an urban area for
more than seventy-two hours unless he complies with certain
conditions, one of which exempts him if he has lawfully
'remained' continuously in that area for not less than fifteen
years! This insecurity is well illustrated by the case of *Regina* v.
Silinga.[1] There, the appellant, an African woman, was convicted for remaining for more than seventy-two hours in an
urban area of the Cape Peninsula. She was ordered to be
removed to the Transkei. She appealed against the conviction,
but not the removal order. The appeal was dismissed by the
Cape Provincial Division of the Supreme Court. On appeal to
the Appellate Division, however, she succeeded. She relied on
the fact that she had been continuously resident in the particular
area by reason of the exemption in section 10(1)(b). The Cape
Provincial Division held against her because she had picked
grapes outside the area from Mondays to Fridays by way of
employment in the years 1947 and 1948, though returning to
her home in the proclaimed area each week-end. It took her the
costs of an appeal to the highest court of the land to establish
her right to remain.[2]

(b) *Specific restrictions enforced extrajudicially by way of preventive
measure or penalty for political thought or action*

The laws which authorize the imposition of specific restrictions on a person's liberty of movement by administrative
order now cover a wide field. We have chosen the following
for discussion:

(i) The Suppression of Communism Act, 1950. Act No. 44
of 1950, as amended.

(ii) The Native Laws Amendment Act, 1952. Act No. 54 of
1952, as amended.

(iii) The Natives (Urban Areas) Amendment Act, 1956. Act
No. 69 of 1956.

[1] 1957 (3) S.A. 354.   [2] Ib. at 357 F–H.

(iv) The Native Administration Amendment Act, 1956. Act No. 42 of 1956.
(v) The Riotous Assemblies Act, 1956. Act No. 17 of 1956.
(vi) The Departure from the Union Regulation Act, 1955. Act No. 34 of 1955.

(i) *The Suppression of Communism Act*, 1950. *No. 44 of* 1950.

As pointed out in an earlier chapter, power by section 10(1) of this Act has been conferred upon the Minister of Justice to banish from a stated area any person whom he is satisfied is in that area advocating, advising, defending, or encouraging the achievement of any of the objects of communism or any act or omission which is *calculated* to further the achievements of any such object, or who is *likely* in any area to advocate, advise, defend, or encourage the achievement of any such object or any such act or omission. When it is considered that the word 'communism' in the Act bears a widely extended meaning, and that subsections (*a*) and (*b*) of section 11 of the Act make it a criminal offence to perform any act which is *calculated* to further the achievement of *any* of the objects of communism, it will be seen that the power in section 10(1) contains a most serious threat to personal liberty. If we assume in favour of this legislation the need for prohibitions against activity included in the statutory definition of communism, and the need for suitable criminal penalties, why was it not possible to make the exercise of the wide discretionary power conferred on the Minister dependent upon a prior conviction under section 11(*a*) or (*b*), or upon a prior conviction for some similar declared offence? That would, of course, have removed from the Minister the power of deciding himself on any information he chose to accept, whether admissible as evidence in a court of law or not, that a person was advocating the achievement of any of the objects of communism. It would also have removed the uncertainty which presents itself to every unconventional political reformer in the Union, namely, whether, perchance, his scheme of reform might not be such as to satisfy the Minister (even if it might never satisfy a court of law) that the achievement of the objects of statutory communism were in fact being advocated thereby.

This much is abundantly evident. The power in this subsection is capable of being used not only to suppress the dangerous doctrines of communism but also to crush political opponents whose acts or political thinking in the sole opinion of the Minister are unacceptable. Indeed, the mere presence in any area of a person deemed by the Governor-General to be a 'communist'[1] could be sufficient grounds for satisfying the Minister that such a person is likely to advocate, etc., the achievement of the objects of 'communism'. The Minister is the sole judge and there is no appeal from any banishing order which he might issue. It is often said that the power is exercised bona fide and with restraint. It may be, but the truth of that assertion, like the Minister's discretion, can never be tested in the searching scrutiny of the courts. Subsection 1(*b*) of section 10 of the Act[2] compels the Minister at the request of the banishing person to supply his reasons for the order, and *so much of the information which induced the Minister to issue the notice as can in his opinion be disclosed without detriment to public policy*. Since the whole of the information upon which the Minister acts in banishing a person need not be disclosed, it becomes impossible to demonstrate that an order was issued mala fide or for a purpose ulterior to the Act, and it is only in such an instance that the courts would interfere. Indeed, even if the information actually disclosed were considered by a court insufficient to warrant the Minister's reasons, it would still not interfere, because that part which is undisclosed might well justify the Minister's reasons and the assumption the courts make is that the Minister has acted for adequate reasons.[3] Thus by a semblance of deference to the principle of *audi alteram partem* this type of legislation satisfies the less critical consciences among us, while at the same time abating no whit from the naked power of arbitrary banishment. Where the subject's home, employment, business, or profession so depend upon the opinion of one officer of the government, the mordant disease of arbitrary rule has surely bitten deep into the liberties of the subject.

It should be observed in conclusion that subsection (3) of section 10 authorizes any commissioned officer of the police to

---

[1] Act 44 of 1950, sec. 1(1)(iii).

[2] Introduced by Act 15 of 1954, sec. 7.

[3] A curious assumption to the layman, since reports of cases in the press frequently disclose executive action to be grounded on inadequate reasons.

cause to be removed from any area any person who has received a banishment order and has failed after seven days to observe it. The act of removal is purely administrative and is not dependent upon a prior conviction of the person under section 11(i) for ignoring the order. The police officer therefore acts without warrant of arrest.

(ii) *The Native Laws Amendment Act*, 1952. *No.* 54 *of* 1952

Section 20 of the above-mentioned Act substitutes a new section 5 in the Native Administration Act of 1927 (No. 38 of 1927). Subsection (1)(*b*) of section 5 authorizes the Governor-General, whenever he deems it expedient in the general public interest, to order a tribe or an African to withdraw from any place to any other place, district, or province within the Union and not to return, *at any time thereafter* or during a specified period, to the former place without the written permission of the Secretary for Native Affairs. It is an offence punishable now with a fine of £50 or imprisonment with or without the option of a fine, to disobey any such order.[1] A conviction for disobeying is no longer, as it was in the original section 5 of Act 38 of 1927, a prerequisite for the African's removal. He may now be summarily arrested and removed without trial on the Governor-General's order to that effect.[2] In effect the order is that of the Cabinet on the application of the Minister of Native Affairs.

No interdict staying the order or the removal may now be granted by any court, and the noting of an appeal against a conviction for disobeying any order does not suspend the operation of the order.[3] Prior to Act 54 of 1952 it was possible under the old section 5 to invoke the aid of interdict procedure. Exemption from laws specially affecting Africans confers no immunity from this type of banishment.

The administrative banishment permitted by this legislation is dependent solely on the Governor-General's deeming it expedient in the general public interest. There is some semblance of control by Parliament in the case of banishment of a tribe, but none in relation to individual Africans. The Governor-General is the sole judge of the public's interests

---

[1] Act 38 of 1927, sec. 5, subsec. 2(*a*) as substituted by Act 54 of 1952, sec. 20.
[2] Ib., sec. 5, subsec. (3). [3] Ib., sec. 5, subsec. (4).

and the expediency of the banishment. The power is a despotic
one even in the hands of a benevolent despot.

The power is not a new one, since it first appeared in Act 38
of 1927. Always arbitrary by nature it has recently acquired
the new features already mentioned, namely, arrest and
removal without prior conviction and immunity from interdict
procedure. The facts of *Lengisi's* case offer a good example of
how the power of banishment under the Act operates.[1] Lengisi
was born in the Sitholeni Location in the district of Engcobo,
Transkei. Prior to 6 July 1954 he had resided for some years in
the Duncan Village Location in East London. He was ordered
by the Governor-General to withdraw from the Duncan Village
Location in East London and to remove and reside at the farm
Schoemansdal No. 13 in the district of Barberton in the Eastern
Transvaal—a very great distance from his earlier residence.
The law report of this case deals solely with the question of the
validity of the order. The merits were of course beside the
point since the court's jurisdiction on this aspect is ousted by
the legislation.

An amendment to section 5(1)(*b*) in 1956 relieves the
Governor-General of the need to give prior notice to the person
banished, thus eliminating prior to banishment the equitable
common law principle which the courts apply even to legislation of this character—*audi alteram partem*.[2] This principle
was applied in *Saliwa's* case by the Court to set aside a banishment order issued without first giving Saliwa the opportunity
of showing cause against.[3] The amendment overcomes, in so far
as notice is concerned, the inconvenience of that beneficial
common law principle. Unlike the Suppression of Communism
Act, which requires at least seven days to elapse before the
order to remove is enforced, a notice issued under section 5(1)(*b*)
of Act 38 of 1927 can compel the African affected to remove
forthwith. No period of grace is apparently regarded as necessary by the legislation to enable the African to settle his affairs.
Of course the Minister may still allow this. He is however not
bound to do so. A further amendment in 1956 also requires the
Minister to furnish an African required to remove with the

[1] *Lengisi* v. *Minister of Native Affairs & another*, 1956 (1) S.A. 786.
[2] Act 42 of 1956, sec. 3(*a*). *Mabe* v. *Minister of Native Affairs*, 1957 (3) S.A. 293.
[3] *Saliwa* v. *Minister of Native Affairs*, 1956 (2) S.A. 310.

reasons for the order and so much of the information which induced the Governor-General to issue the order as can in the Minister's opinion be disclosed without detriment to the public interest.[1] We have seen, however, that this obligation provides little, if any, protection.

(iii) *The Natives (Urban Areas) Amendment Act*, 1956. *No.* 69 *of* 1956

Legislation dealing with Africans in the urban areas of the Union has for many years conferred the power on a magistrate or Native commissioner to adjudge Africans 'idle and disorderly' after due notice and inquiry, and to order the removal from the urban area where he is at the time of any such African, who may also be ordered not to return to that urban area.[2] The magistrate so adjudging him may also commit him to a farm or work colony or similar institution for a period not exceeding two years. This procedure follows upon complaint and proof that the African in question is habitually unemployed or has no sufficient honest means of livelihood, or is leading an idle and disorderly life, and on several other grounds not important to the principle mentioned. The power can involve extremely severe consequences for such an African. Cases have occurred where Africans have been debarred from returning to an urban area for periods up to ten years. A right of appeal and review to the Supreme Court lies against any order committing an African so adjudged to a work colony, farm colony, refuge, or rescue home. It does not appear that any appeal or review is given against a simple removal order.[3]

In 1956 however a far-reaching encroachment on civil liberty was enacted in the provisions of section 1 of Act 69 of 1956.[4] The effect of this section is to empower an urban local authority to banish any African from its area of jurisdiction if *in its opinion* the presence of that African is 'detrimental to the

---

[1] Act 42 of 1956, sec. 3(*b*). The principle of *audi alteram partem* is not entirely precluded because it seems that the Minister is obliged, after supplying his reasons (when requested to do so) to consider any representation made at this late stage. *Mabe's* case, *supra*, at 299 C.

[2] Act 21 of 1923, sec. 17. Act 25 of 1945, sec. 29, as substituted by Act 54 of 1952, sec. 36.

[3] Act 25 of 1945, sec. 29(10).

[4] Introducing a new section, 29(*bis*), into the Natives (Urban Areas) Consolidation Act, No. 25 of 1945.

maintenance of peace and good order' in its area or any part thereof.

It is worthy of notice that what was previously necessary in adjudging an African to be idle and disorderly, namely, complaint, notice and due inquiry before a judicial officer, is not requited for the more important banishment order by a town council under section 29(*bis*) of Act 25 of 1945 as amended. In the latter case there is no inquiry at which the person concerned is faced with a complaint and information on which it is based. He can be adjudged by the local authority in his absence, on evidence or information he has no right to challenge by cross-examination. This procedure, it appears, applies to an African who has been born and domiciled in an urban area as well as to one who is domiciled outside such an area. It does not depend upon anti-social conduct such as vagrancy or habitual unemployment. The banishment may be permanent or temporary. It can however be used as a weapon against the African who agitates for improved transport facilities or better housing, or who opposes his womenfolk's being required to carry identity documents. Here then is another example of the cancer which is eating away the rule of law—the grant to town councils of the arbitrary power to destroy an African's home and his means of providing for his family if he should become troublesome to municipal government, through conduct, it should be emphasized, not necessarily involving any contravention of the law.

No appeal lies against such a banishment order.[1] It is a terrible and destructive power to rest untrammelled and without appeal in local authority government. By-laws regulating the most trifling affairs of civic life require the approval of the

[1] The Minister said in the House of Assembly on 11 June 1956 (*Hansard*, cols. 7394–6) that an African can appeal against the *verdict* before the removal order can be carried out, as this is subsequent to the payment of any fine or serving of any sentence imposed. (Appeal could be to the Supreme Court in the normal way.) Should he appeal, the merits of his case and of the issuing of the removal order would be investigated, the Minister said. But this is merely an appeal against the conviction for failing to obey the order of the town council. It is *not* an appeal against the town council's order, and the Minister's statement that the merits of the removal order would be investigated appears to be incorrect. All the court on appeal would inquire into would be whether in fact the town council came to the necessary opinion requisite for the application of the section, not whether it correctly did so.

Administrator. No safeguard at all is required when a town council banishes an African under section 29(*bis*) and deprives him of his home and his means of earning a living in its area. It must make a report to the Minister of its action, who must in turn lay a copy of this report on the table of both Houses of Parliament. Permission to re-enter granted by the council can countermand the banishment. Town councils are not always inhibited by considerations of equity and restraint—witness the unjust and shameless proposals made by some councils to the Group Areas Board, reference to which has been made in Chapter II.

(iv) *The Native Administration Amendment Act*, 1956. *No. 42 of* 1956

This Act extends the wide powers which the Governor-General, as Supreme Chief, holds over Africans in Natal, the Transvaal, and the Orange Free State, to the Cape Province, a curious reversion to outmoded methods of government in the case of an African community which until 1936 had enjoyed the common-roll franchise since the early days of Cape rule under the Crown—a community which moreover has been longer in touch with Western civilization than any other Africans in the subcontinent.

The important and direct result of this anomaly is that Africans who in the past were considered fit to enjoy the franchise on the common roll now find themselves governed by a code of 'Native law' which permits the Supreme Chief, that is, the Governor-General, to punish them for disobedience to administrative orders without the intervention of the courts, and in certain circumstances without even an administrative hearing. This system of law permits the arrest and confinement of Africans at any time, and they have no legal recourse to the principle of *habeas corpus*. Although the Governor-General is the Supreme Chief, the Act is administered by the Minister of Native Affairs, and power therefore really resides in him. (This matter is dealt with more fully in Chapter XII).

(v) *The Riotous Assemblies Act*, 1956. *No. 17 of* 1956

The power of administrative banishment, which is a recurring feature in South African legislation in the last few years, appears again in section 3(5) of the above-mentioned Act.

It first appeared in 1930.[1] Under section 3(5) of Act 17 of 1956 the Minister may, by notice delivered to any person, prohibit him from being within any area defined in the notice, whenever *he is satisfied* that such person is promoting feelings of hostility between the European inhabitants of the Union on the one hand and any other section of the inhabitants on the other hand. Failure to observe such a notice is an offence and is punishable with a sentence of imprisonment not exceeding three months, and on a second conviction not exceeding six months. The person served with a notice may be removed after the expiration of seven days by any member of the police acting without judicial warrant, and independently of a conviction for failing to observe the notice. The Minister is given a discretion to pay the person's expenses of removal if he so desires.

The Appellate Division described a similar power conferred by Act 19 of 1930 as follows:

There is no doubt the Act gives the Minister a discretion of a wide and drastic kind and one which, in its exercise, must necessarily make a serious inroad upon the ordinary liberty of the subject. Its object is clear, it is to stop at the earliest possible stage the fomentation of feelings of hostility between the European and non-European sections of the community.[2]

There can be little doubt that circumstances are conceivable where the exercise of such a drastic power would be called for. The purpose of including it here is to offer one more illustration of the extent to which Parliament has gone in committing to executive officials the political weapon of banishment. The moral purpose of the Act as set out above one can approve, but that should not prevent us from appreciating the dangers it conceals. Practically any agitation for reform in the Union in the interests of unskilled labour could be construed as a fomentation of hostility against the European. He is of the governing community from whom the reform must come, and the person who seeks the reform is usually of the non-governing and voteless section of the community—the non-European. The clash of interest in this situation might well produce

---

[1] Act 19 of 1930, sec. 1, inserting the power into Act 27 of 1914 as sec. 1(12).
[2] *Sacks* v. *Minister of Justice*, 1934 A.D. 11 at 36.

hostility—the political hostility of any section of society which has less privileges than another—the same hostility which the artisan classes of Britain felt during the Industrial Revolution for the wealthier classes employing them. To prohibit the promotion of hostility in these circumstances is virtually to prohibit any activity which presses for reform, for representations for reform may well, if they go unheeded, result in hostility. The danger of legislation of this character is its ready availability to abuse. Agitation engendering hostility to essentially economic and social forces can in a multiracial community where privilege rests mainly in one race so easily be interpreted as agitation, promoting hostility based on racial grounds. It may have nothing to do with the latter, though in its result it affects a racial class. It is easy in these circumstances to categorize the activity under section 3(5) in order to remove political opponents whose activities are grounded on economic and social pressures not unique to the Union.

(vi) *The Departure from the Union Regulation Act*, 1955. *No.* 34 *of* 1955

The right in times of peace to travel beyond the borders of one's own country has never been questioned in countries enjoying parliamentary institutions, until quite recently, when it has, in the Union, been made a crime to leave the country without a travel document of some kind authorizing that departure. The issue of a passport, though in general subject to the discretion of the government of a State, has not been a prerequisite for a subject's departure from his own country.

In 1955 the Union Parliament enacted the law mentioned above, the effect of which was to prohibit anyone from leaving the Union if he was not in possession of a valid passport or permit. No South African, even if of dual nationality, that is, even if a citizen also of the United Kingdom and holding a passport of that country, may leave without a South African passport or, in the case of the last-mentioned, without a South African permit *in addition to* his United Kingdom passport.

In explaining the object of the Bill, the Minister stated that it was aimed at stopping the spread of communism. Prior to the Act a number of people to whom South African passports had been denied had left the Union without them, as they were then entitled to do. When overseas they secured travel documents from foreign countries—in some cases the Soviet Union —permitting their travelling unhampered by the absence of a South African passport. *En passant* it is to be noted that the possession of a South African passport is now in some countries a cause of embarrassment, for example in India. A case comes to mind of a South African citizen who, desiring to visit relatives in India, has been compelled to live in the Central African Federation for a period in order to qualify for a passport of that country and then to visit his relations. In this case, although the South African passport would probably be available to him, it is no 'open sesame' to travel in India!

The system now in force means that a South African citizen cannot leave his country temporarily for places other than Basutoland, Bechuanaland, or Swaziland, without the permission of his government. If he does he commits an offence punishable with imprisonment of *not less* than three months and not more than two years. There is no option of a fine. Any person conveying such a South African also commits an offence, and is liable to be fined up to £2,000 or to be imprisoned for a period not exceeding one year, or to be both so fined and imprisoned.

An applicant for a passport has no redress if refused. He has no means of knowing on what information the Minister has regarded him as unfit to leave. He cannot therefore meet anything in it which might be adverse to him. Recourse to the courts is not open since a refusal rests in the complete discretion of the Minister. The latter is not even restricted to using it only in the case of persons named under the Suppression of Communism Act, that is, persons of whom it might with some slight semblance of reason be said that their departure and return would assist in the spread of communism. This legislation contains a terrible potential as a weapon against political opponents. Small wonder that the voice of many South Africans is stilled in criticism of their government. It is difficult in many cases to find any links between the reason given by the Minister for the introduction of the law and the actual administration of the Act. Patrick Duncan, son of a former Governor-General of the Union, a member of the Liberal Party and an outspoken critic of the present government, was recently refused a passport. No reasons were given and none need be. There is here no provision similar to that in other legislation already discussed, requiring the Minister to state his reasons when called upon by the person affected. While regulations in the United States control the issue of passports on grounds affecting communism, it is noteworthy that it is still not an offence to leave that country, even if the destination be Soviet Russia, without such a passport, however inconvenient such a course might actually prove.[1]

The foregoing constitute some of the restrictions which have multiplied so rapidly during the last few years to confine the subject's freedom of movement both inside and outside his own country. Other instances there doubtless are, but the list is a sorry enough one already.

It is time to conclude this subject, and it would not be inapt to do so with some excerpts from a speech in 1934 made by General Smuts in a world context pregnant with the rise of Nazism:

Individual freedom, individual independence of mind, individual participation in the difficult work of government seem to me essential to all true progress. . . . There is decay in principle which is eating the very vitals of free government. . . . There is today a decay of the individual's responsibility and share in government, which seems to strike at the roots of our human advance.

Freedom is the most ineradicable craving of human nature.

Those words uttered in 1934 carry an ominous and prescient note for our own times!

---

[1] See article in *Annual Survey of South African Law*, 1955, p. 27.

CHAPTER VI

Freedom to Express Opinions

It is a fundamental principle of government based upon the wishes of the governed, that sufficient scope should be allowed the latter to express their opinions.

W. Ivor Jennings in *The Law and the Constitution* says:

There are some rights however which are inherent in a system of government by opinion. For this system implies the right to create opinion and to organize with a view to influencing the conduct of government. There can be no such system if minority opinions cannot be expressed, or if people cannot meet together to discuss their opinions and their actions, or if those who think alike on any subject cannot associate for mutual support and for the propagation of their common ideas.[1]

The same author in another work writes as follows:

Without free elections the people cannot make a choice of policies. Without freedom of speech the appeal to reason which is the basis of democracy cannot be made. Without freedom of association electors and elected representatives cannot band themselves into parties for the formulation of common policies and the attainment of common ends.[2]

This chapter is concerned, in the main, with the civil liberty involved in the freedom to express opinions, whether by the spoken or written word, but it will be necessary to touch upon some subjects closely allied, for example, association for the purposes of discussion, and access to written matter and news influencing thought and discussion.

It is necessary also, at the outset, to clarify our approach to the subject. The phrase 'right to freedom of speech' is often loosely used in the sense of conveying that the constitution in some way guarantees and entrenches that right.[3] In what

---

[1] 3rd ed., p. 236.   [2] *Cabinet Government* (1936), p. 13.

[3] 'Die Wet maak 'n ernstige inbreuk op die regte van die landsburgers. Vryheid van spreuk en vrydom van die burger is hoekstene van ons grondwet,' de Villiers, J., in *du Plessis* v. *Minister of Justice*, 1950 (3) S.A. at 581, in reference to Act 27 of 1914, sec. 1(7), as amended (the Riotous Assemblies Act).

follows we use the phrase. however, as signifying a logical and generally admitted political principle of free government, since in the Union as in Great Britain the so-called 'right' is no more than the right to express opinions where that act is not prohibited or restricted by the law of the country. Thus, anything may be said or written which it is not illegal under the laws of the Union to say or write. The 'right' in this sense is liable to be whittled away by Parliament, indeed, even to the point where it is extinguished. For these reasons the discussion of this freedom is here based on the use of the terms 'freedom of speech' or 'freedom to criticize' in the sense of a basic political principle of free and democratic government, and the inquiry is directed to ascertaining the extent to which that desirable principle of government is receiving recognition in the Union.

The 'right' is of course not an absolute one. Qualification of the principle is necessary in the interest both of the State and fellow subjects. The law penalizes libel and slander, seditious speeches, and writings. But, accepting the need for qualification, few imbued with notions of free government will dispute that a just recognition of the principle in a country claiming to administer democratic government requires as little encroachment as possible upon freedom of speech consistent with the maintenance of public order, security, and the private rights of other subjects. Every qualification beyond these bounds destroys the hypothesis upon which the parliamentary system works. In the Union, where a minority of the population has effective control of the government, the need for a minimum of restriction upon the expression of opinions by the voteless majority hardly requires emphasis. Of the steadily shrinking and now limited facilities available to that majority for making its opinions known within Parliament, mention will be made later (Chapter XI). We are interested here, rather in the operation of the freedom to criticize in the extra-parliamentary field.

The claim has been made by some critics of the South African government that its powers are so wide that it can permanently silence the voice of opposition. Let us examine the truth or otherwise of this assertion by looking into the armoury of the government and at some of the formidable weapons of repression that lie ready to its hand if it be minded to use them.

One of the most potent factors operating upon the actions of governments throughout the world today is the force of world opinion. Few states relish being arraigned before that tribunal. Where this is ranged against any government, the latter's task of persuading its subjects to support policies, widely condemned in the world outside as contrary to the conscience of civilized mankind, becomes infinitely difficult. There is however the expedient of shutting off the minds of its subjects from the full impact of world opinion by censorship. The South African government is of course not unique in prohibiting the importation of literature which is subversive to the State.

Where it excludes literature outside this category and damaging to its philosophy of white supremacy, it is on less common and justifiable ground. Anything strongly educative of public opinion in the direction of a common society in the Union, or critical of the government's racial attitudes, runs the risk of being banned under the Customs Act, No. 55 of 1955, which in addition to censorship on the usual ground of public morals permits political censorship at the discretion of the Minister on the broad and vague ground of reading-matter being 'objectionable'.

But the use of this weapon in impeding freedom to criticize is available only against imported matter. Because no powers of direct control exist over the Union's press, the broad stream of world opinion continues to have its educative influence upon the South African public. Something more is needed if the curtain is to be effectively drawn between external influences and the South African public, and the only remaining step possible is some form of censorship of local matter.

It is not surprising therefore to see that a recently appointed government commission conducting its investigations under the title of the Undesirable Publications Commission has produced a plan for censorship of books, newspapers, and other publications. While this weapon against freedom to express opinion is not yet in the armoury, the possibility of its manufacture and inclusion is sufficiently real to warrant a reference to the plan. A thorough reading of the Commission's report will dispel any illusions as to its ultimate purpose. Under colour of a need to deal with the problem of pornographic and horror literature, the Commission clearly envisages an extension of censorship into the political field.

The report recommends that control over publications should be vested in two authorities. A 'Publications Board' appointed by the government will decide what books, magazines, and other publications are undesirable. Newspapers will be subject to the jurisdiction of the courts, which will act within the definitions and conditions laid down by legislation.

Printed matter is to be regarded as undesirable if it is deemed indecent, offensive, or *harmful* by the ordinary civilized, decent, reasonable, and responsible inhabitant of the Union. As the commissioners doubtless place themselves in this latter category, a sample of what such a person's standards are is supplied by the suggestions in the report, which, in the main, even in detailed wording, are those prevalent among members of the present government.[1] There is much evidence that what it regards as 'harmful' to the South African public is identical with anything strongly critical of the government's policies.

The Commission's plan is still of course only in the recommendation stage. In the context, however, of the prevailing intolerance on the part of the authorities towards views based on a philosophy of race relations other than its own, and the only partial success of its many other steps to reduce the voice of criticism, this final step towards direct censorship of political opinion seems a logical one for it to take. Particularly is this the case when it is remembered that a Commission inquiring into the Press of the Union will be delivering its report in the not distant future.

In the present absence of a direct censorship of public opinion, what else is capable of being used to impede or threaten the free expression of that opinion?

Section 6(*d*) of the Suppression of Communism Act provides that:

If the Governor-General is satisfied that any periodical or other publication serves *inter alia* as a means for expressing views or conveying information, the publication of which is calculated to further

[1] See para. 5: 93 of the report for details.

the achievement of any of the objects of communism, he may, without notice to any person concerned, by proclamation in the *Gazette* prohibit the printing, publication or dissemination of such periodical publication or the dissemination of such other publication. . . .[1]

When it is remembered that many of the reforms now advocated in the Union in a constitutional spirit could without difficulty be equated with *some* of the aims of communism, as indeed they could with some of the aims of Christian teaching, the damaging effect of this wide administrative power upon the free expression of opinion can hardly be doubted. There is the ever-present uncertainty that some forthright and advanced advocacy of reform in the leader column might transgress that vague and undefined boundary line which, in the Minister's sole opinion, places the writing in the category mentioned in section 6(*d*). Free and courageous expression of criticism is hardly likely to flourish in a climate so loaded with the ominous clouds of administrative disapproval and penalty.

The individual fares no better than the press. If his expressed views carry him too far he might find that he has advocated, advised, defended, or encouraged the achievement of some object of or some act *calculated* to further the achievement of an object of communism, though having done so in a completely constitutional and proper manner, and with the object of producing normal and regular democratic reform. Doubtless the ideal of equal opportunity to fill skilled posts irrespective of the colour of the workman is one of the objects of communism. Many a conventional politician would be outraged to find that if he advocated reform along the lines of that principle he could be regarded as encouraging the achievement of one of the objects of communism. Yet the Act permits his being dealt with as a 'communist' with all the serious consequences already mentioned in Chapters II and V. Not even the privilege accorded to members of Parliament in the debates in the House will protect him as a member of Parliament from being so deemed. He can be as effectively silenced by the penalties of the Act as if the grave had closed over him.

That a number of prominent liberal reformers continue, though not without wariness, to express opinions which are

[1] Act 44 of 1950, sec. 6, as amended by Act 50 of 1951, sec. 5.

anathema to the government is sometimes advanced as proof that freedom of speech has in fact not been impaired. It is pertinent however to inquire whether less prominent figures could do so with impunity. Could any member of the African National Congress do so? Or any African? Assuming it were possible to do so and come through unscathed, the real test is surely whether the measure produces a state of mind in the ordinary citizen which substantially affects the free expression of his opinions. There can be little doubt that on this test the South African public today refrains from public political comment. There is too great a risk that any such comment will, in the minds of the government, be regarded as indiscreet and perhaps worse. Total abstinence from an activity so fraught with risk is preferable to the alternatives!

During 1952 a passive-resistance movement against discriminatory laws based on race developed in the Union. Its principal protagonists were Africans and Indians, though a few cases of European participation occurred. The problem of countless numbers of black beople contravening the laws of the country in protest and willingly submitting to imprisonment, presented the government with a situation which might well have produced the breakdown of these laws. Faced with this, it enacted with the help of the main opposition party, the Criminal Law Amendment Act, 1953. This act prescribed increased penalties for contraventions of the country's laws when these infringements occurred by way of protest or in support of any campaign against or for the repeal, modification, or variation or limitation of the application or administration of any law.[1]

Harsh penalties including a whipping could be imposed even for a first offence. Other offences were created by the Act but the right to criticize or campaign for the repeal of or modification of the country's laws by pure discussion and persuasion remained, though not without the addition of some further risk to those who exercised that right. The additional risk is latent in the wide provisions of section 2(b) of the Act which reads as follows:

Any person who . . . uses any language or does any act or thing *calculated* to cause any person or persons in general to commit an

[1] Act 8 of 1953, sec. 1.

offence by way of protest against a law or in support of any campaign for the repeal or modification of any law or the variation or limitation of the application or administration of any law shall be guilty of an offence and liable upon conviction to

(i)   a fine not exceeding £500; or
(ii) imprisonment for a period not exceeding five years; or
(iii) a whipping not exceeding 10 strokes; or
(iv) both such fine and such imprisonment; or
(v)   both such fine and such whipping; or
(vi) both such imprisonment and such a whipping.

Provided that in the case of a second or subsequent conviction it shall not be competent to impose a fine except in conjunction with whipping or imprisonment.

An indignant and legitimate protest in a leader column against a harsh or absurd law might well be calculated to cause members of the public to break that law by way of protest, quite independently of and contrary to the intention of the writer. An unfair and unwarranted restriction upon or interference with property rights, or an unjust tax, in each case imposed by a municipality, has been known to call forth indignant protests and invitations to disregard the law from prominent burgesses and the press; a refusal, in protest, to pay a garden-hose licence—all these fall within the rigour of this harsh law. A minister of the church, counselling his flock to continue their worship in his church in protest against the recent law empowering the Minister of Native Affairs to prohibit joint worship by Europeans and Africans in urban areas, would render himself liable to suffer the penalty *inter alia* of a whipping of ten strokes.

Small wonder that the enactment of this law has caused the press and individuals to be extremely guarded in their protests. That these conditions have inhibited freedom of discussion and speech is certain. Direct censorship of political opinion becomes an unnecessary and clumsy weapon with which to silence criticism, when by indirect means such as these such an atmosphere of caution and fear is infused that the voice of public protest, although not silenced, ceases to have that clarion note of warning that is necessary where fundamental liberties are threatened. 'If the trumpet sound an uncertain note who shall prepare himself for battle?'

The armoury of repressive legislation aimed at free expression of opinion is, however, by no means exhausted with these measures. One, more comprehensive than any of them, and striking ultimately more deeply at the heart of the public's liberties, passed Parliament in 1953, with the aid of the main opposition party. True, the Public Safety Act (No. 3 of 1953) is primarily designed to meet a situation of crisis and emergency, where the safety of the public or the maintenance of public order is seriously threatened, and similar legislation exists in countries following the Western parliamentary tradition. The only safeguard against an abuse of the extremely wide powers vested in the government by this class of legislation is, of course, good sense and restraint on the part of the Executive, and a vigilant Parliament ready to resume power over the government. We are concerned here with the extent of the powers to suppress criticism and not with the merits or otherwise of such legislation. The potentiality of its use is a sufficient threat.

We pass now to a discussion of the Riotous Assemblies Act.[1] Section 3(1) reads as follows:

Whenever the Governor-General is of the opinion that the publication or other dissemination of any documentary information is calculated to engender feelings of hostility between the European inhabitants of the Union on the one hand and any other section of the inhabitants of the Union on the other hand, he may by notice published in the *Gazette* and in any newspaper circulating in the area where that documentary information is made available to the public, prohibit any publication or other dissemination thereof.

This provision first made its appearance in 1930 during the term of office of the Nationalist government of General Hertzog.[2] Reference has been made in Chapter V to the provisions of the Act in relation to freedom of movement. Restrictions imposed on freedom of movement under the Act inevitably flow from an exercise of the right of freedom of speech. The subject brings himself within the main prohibitions of the Act

---

[1] Act 17 of 1956, repealing previous legislation of this character, the first Act being No. 27 of 1914.

[2] Act 19 of 1930, sec. 1, inserting a new subsec. (7) into sec. 1, Act 27 of 1914 (the original Riotous Assemblies Act).

by conduct calculated to promote feelings of hostility between white and non-white people.

It is to be observed that the provisions quoted above do not produce a subjective test of intent as in section 29(1) of Act 38 of 1927 (the Native Administration Act), which reads as follows:

Any person who utters words or does any other act or thing what-ever *with intent* to promote any feeling of hostility between Natives and Europeans shall be guilty of an offence and liable on con-viction to imprisonment for a period not exceeding one year or to a fine of one hundred pounds or both.

Suppose that someone bona fide believes that a certain state of affairs constitutes a social disease requiring drastic reform and campaigns against this evil. He might well use language which is likely to inflame feelings of hostility on the part of the Africans against the persons responsible for the state of affairs. If his language be strong, if his intentions be purely constitu-tional methods of reform, he runs the risk of action being taken against him under the Riotous Assemblies Act should his words be *calculated* to promote hostility between white and non-white.[1]

A Samuel Wilberforce, campaigning today in the Union against some of its social diseases and legislation, could scarcely avoid falling foul of this provision of the law though his intention might be far removed from that of promoting hostility.

As pointed out in Chapter V, the social and economic situation in the Union is such that vigorous and constitutional denunciation of social evils and agitation for reform are quite capable of arousing a class hostility between privileged and less privileged, between those against whom discrimination operates and those against whom it does not. The two classes broadly coincide with a classification of the population on racial lines

---

[1] See the remarks of Murray, J., in *Rex* v. *Sutherland & others*, 1950 (4) S.A. at 71, a case on the provisions of sec. 29(1) of Act 38 of 1927, an extract of which appears in the text above, which unlike the Riotous Assemblies Act requires proof of a specific *intent* to promote hostility. It was because the Crown failed to estab-lish this intent that the accused in *Sutherland's* case, who were representatives of the *Sunday Express*, which published a cartoon attacking Dr. Malan's invitation to the British protectorates in South Africa to enter the Union, were acquitted. The case offers an excellent example of bona fide comment on public issues, freedom to express which should not be hampered by laws such as those under discussion.

of white and non-white. Criticism based on principles of social and economic reform can without difficulty therefore be stigmatized as calculated to promote hostility on racial lines. Some safeguard, however, does exist against the possible abuse of subsection (1) of section 3, in the provision that any person affected by a prohibition imposed in terms of that subsection may apply to the Supreme Court to set aside the prohibition. The onus is however on him, if he does so, to prove that the publication is not calculated to have that result.[1]

Freedom of speech is further subjected to the risks involved in contravening section 17 of the new Act, which penalizes anyone for the crime of incitement to public violence if in any place whatever he has acted or conducted himself in such a manner or has spoken or published such words that it might reasonably be expected that the natural and probable consequences of his act, conduct, speech or publication would under the circumstances be the commission of public violence by members of the public generally, or by persons in whose presence the act or conduct took place or to whom the speech or publication was addressed.

With these possibilities in mind both the individual and the press must necessarily exercise warily the right to express opinions, with a caution which cannot be healthy and conducive to a proper working of parliamentary government. It is admittedly difficult to preserve law and order without some control of this nature. Nevertheless, the Act casts so wide a net that a large class of legitimate and constitutional criticism is in practice eliminated from the processes of government. One is perhaps permitted to ask why the less restrictive prohibition (one dependent upon intent) contained in section 29(1) of Act 38 of 1927 (the Native Administration Act) could not be the criterion for excluding matter which offends against the preserving of good race relations. Again the procedure adopted in Great Britain of binding over a person to be of good behaviour might usefully be substituted, where evidence exists from, say, past statements or writings that the offence might again be committed. While we are on the subject, we should not lose sight of the fact that much of the legislation based on compul-

[1] Act 17 of 1956, sec. 3(3).

sory apartheid is itself of a character disruptive of good race
relations, and violates the very principle which the Act seeks
to safeguard. There are few cases where Europeans have been
prosecuted for words calculated to promote the hostility of
Europeans against non-Europeans. Yet anyone who has had
experience of South African elections will find it hard to believe
that conduct of this nature is unknown.

Freedom to express opinions depends in a large measure upon
facilities to assemble and to discuss matters of common interest.
In the past few years, legislation, in the form of municipal by-
laws as well as regulations,[1] has made its appearance, the effect
of which has been to subject meetings, in both public and
private places, to the permission of the local authority concerned. After the case of *Arenstein* v. *Durban Corporation*[2] had set
aside as *ultra vires* a by-law of the Durban Corporation which
conferred discretion on the mayor to authorize or prohibit any
procession, display, or gathering in any public place, this type
of legislation has been modified to make it slightly less authoritarian in character. But the difficulties in the way of inter-
racial gatherings created by municipal restriction are still
substantial.

An example of these is given by the case of *Rex* v. *Seedat &*
another.[3]

The promoters of a Colonial Youth Day meeting, sponsored
by the African National Congress Youth League and the Natal
Indian Youth Congress, were charged with contravening a
Durban by-law by holding a meeting in a public place without
the mayor's consent. This charge failed on the ground that the
meeting was in fact held on private property. An alternative
charge, however, succeeded, the gravamen of which was that
the meeting had been held without giving due notice to the
mayor as required by regulation 8 read with regulation 13 of
the city council's regulations.[4]

The relevant regulations are as follows:

8. No person shall attend or take part in any meeting or assembly
of natives for any other purpose than a *dance, game* or *entertainment*

---

[1] Made under the powers conferred on local authorities by sec. 38(3)(r) of
Act 25 of 1945 (the Natives [Urban Areas] Consolidation Act).
[2] 1952 (1) S.A. 279 (A.D.)   [3] 1957 (1) S.A. 27 (N).
[4] Made in terms of the powers conferred by Act 25 of 1945, sec. 38(3)(r).

in any building or in any public or *private*[1] place within the Borough unless notice has been given by the convener or conveners of such meeting or assembly at least seventy-two hours before the time at which it is proposed to hold such meeting or assembly to the Mayor of Durban, or in his absence to the Deputy Mayor and his consent obtained thereto.

... 13. Every person who shall attend or take part in any meeting or assembly of Natives of which notice in terms of these regulations has not been given or which has been prohibited by the Mayor in terms of these regulations or who shall conduct himself in disorderly manner at any such meeting or assembly shall be guilty of an offence.

Regulation 10 authorizes the mayor, 'with the official approval of the magistrate after reference to the local police and the location manager', to 'prohibit the holding of such meeting if there be reasonable grounds for believing that the holding of such meeting may provoke or tend to a breach of the peace'.

It is apparent from regulation 8 that in the view of the Durban City Council the assembly of Africans for any purpose of an intellectual or serious character, even in a private home, is something that ought not to occur without due notice to the mayor.

Indeed, recently a gathering of people of different races in the library of a Durban college, consisting of well-known and respectable burgesses of the city, resulted in a prosecution and conviction of some of them under this class of regulation. In that instance there was no secrecy about the meeting, which was a public one on private premises, of which ample notice had been given. The circumstances of the meeting so obviously pointed to a lawful and orderly gathering that there was not the slightest ground for apprehending any breach of the peace. It is interesting to observe how a power for municipal purposes, such as regulating and controlling traffic, and the use of streets and public places, has now been extended, and employed to control and suppress political gatherings. It is difficult to find any other reason for the authorities' action in the case cited.

Official powers of impeding free assembly even of a constitutional character are so varied and numerous that the confines

---

[1] The italics are ours.

of this chapter do not permit anything more than the briefest reference to some of these. Mention has already been made in Chapter III of the powers of the police in section 44 of the Criminal Procedure Act of 1955. To this must be added a power under the Riotous Assemblies Act to prohibit public meetings on the ground that they would seriously endanger the public peace, or that feelings of hostility would be engendered between the European inhabitants of the Union on the one hand and any other section of the population on the other.[1]

It is an offence for a person in a Native area, without the permission of the chief or headman if any and of the Native commissioner, and, in any other area, without the permission of the magistrate, to hold, preside at, or address any gathering at which more than ten Africans are present or to permit such a gathering to be held on premises under his control. Certain gatherings are excepted—bona fide religious or funeral services, meetings involving purely domestic affairs, the business of a statutory body, meetings for the purpose of instruction under any law, bona fide sports gatherings or entertainments, weddings, meetings attended by a member of Parliament or of the Provincial Council, and meetings for official administrative purposes. These regulations came into force immediately in 1953 in all Native areas. Elsewhere they operate from a date fixed by the Governor-General.[2]

In 1956 these regulations, as amended, were brought into operation also in the districts of Port Elizabeth and Humansdorp.[3]

In the same year the Governor-General, using his powers under section 27(1) of Act 38 of 1927 (the Native Administration Act) of 'prohibiting, controlling and regulating gatherings of Natives', made regulations for the Evaton area in the Transvaal similar to those mentioned above.[4]

The Native Resettlement Board, established under Act 19 of 1954 to administer the removal of Africans from certain

[1] Act 17 of 1956, sec. 2(1) and (3).
[2] Proclamation No. 198 and Government Notice No. 2017 of the *Government Gazette* No. 5138 of 18 September 1953.
[3] On 2 March 1956 by Government Notice No. 354 of the *Government Gazette* No. 5638 of 2 March 1956.
[4] Government Notice No. 2025, *Government Gazette* No. 5764 of 2 November 1956.

areas in which they had lived in the Johannesburg district to other areas in the district, made regulations in 1956 governing public meetings and assemblies of Africans in the locations under its control on lines similar to those already outlined.[1] Application to the authorities is a *sine qua non* of any meetings under this last-mentioned provision. The nature and purpose of the meeting and the subjects to be discussed must be disclosed in the application. If during the course of the meeting any subject is discussed other than that for which authority has been granted, a member of the police or officer of the Resettlement Board may order an adjournment.

Finally, on this related subject of freedom of assembly, the Minister has the power to prohibit a gathering in any place in the Union, or a person from attending any particular gathering or all gatherings, if in the Minister's opinion the achievement of any of the objects of 'communism', as defined in the wide terms of the Suppression of Communism Act, would be furthered by such meeting or attendance.[2] The considerable number of prosecutions and appeals to superior courts arising from this latter provision testify to the extent to which it is being used, and to the complexity of its provisions.

So much then for the direct methods of restricting the subject's freedom to express his opinion, to criticize, and to assemble for these purposes. It would be idle to pretend that they are not formidable obstacles and deterrents to all but the boldest critics. Mere courage to speak what conscience dictates is, however, not enough, for the casualties in the defence of civil freedom are heavy, and as the iron hand of control tightens fewer recruits are found to join the ranks.

But perhaps a much graver threat to this freedom lies in the indirect and sinister pressures which hide behind direct legislative prohibitions, and emerge in the constant administrative harrying of those who oppose outside the parliamentary field. All the forms of official pressure are brought to bear against any form of joint activity between white and non-white of a political character. Protagonists of a common society are

[1] Government Notice 1924, *Government Gazette* No. 5760 of 26 October 1956. These regulations were made under the Board's powers imposed by sec. 30 of Act 19 of 1954 read with sec. 38(3)(r) and (5) of Act 25 of 1945.

[2] Act 44 of 1950, sec. 9.

treated as enemies of the security of the State. Their public and private meetings, constitutional and of an open character, are attended by members of the Special Security Branch of the police. Notes are taken of their speeches. Where they meet in private homes, the registration numbers of their cars have been taken by the police. An aura of sinister plotting and crime against the security of the State is made by these attentions to hang over their discussions. Photographs are taken of processions or meetings where white and non-white meet together in common interest. The police visit and question these people. Technical breaches of the law, as in the instance of the meeting of people in the Durban college already referred to, where the mayor's consent had not been obtained, are visited with the full rigour of prosecution. In Pietermaritzburg a procession of African women headed by a few European women, proceeding to the Chief Native Commissioner through the streets of the city in an orderly demonstration against passes for African women, resulted in the arrest of 623 women. Longmarket Street was lined at intervals by plain-clothes members of the police force. No untoward incident occurred. Ultimately the charge preferred against the women, one based on a municipal by-law, was withdrawn. In police archives, however, the photographs taken of these women remain as a record demonstrating their opposition to the government's policy of apartheid. No law-abiding citizen will relish that covert threat, and as a result the insidious disease of intimidation and fear works its way deeper into the body politic, to fester there in outraged and wounded feelings.

The facets of administrative intimidation are so varied that it is impossible here to enter into detail. If the reader is interested in probing this matter further he should refer elsewhere.[1] Other chapters mention some of these indirect pressures.[2] The subject is, however, not complete without some reference to the indirect financial pressures which official patronage exerts. Business men, in the main, eschew any form of political activity beyond recording their vote—not so much because of possible

---

[1] See, e.g., 'Is it a Crime to Oppose the Government?' by Alexander Heppel, M.P., in *The Forum*, February 1957.

[2] *Inter alia*, the refusal of passports, and the use of prosecutions under the laws of vehicle registration and transportation in the bus boycott in Johannesburg.

repercussions from their customers, though this is unquestionably a factor in many cases, but also and more often because of those which it is feared might follow from the authorities. Merchants are dependent upon the latter's good will for many concessions and grants, among others import permits for their stock in trade. It may be that their fear on this score is groundless, though instances have been known which have lent some colour to these fears.[1] The fact is, however, that that fear exists as a real one.

Recently the *Natal Mercury* made a public apology to the Speaker of the Assembly for the publication by it of a pungent leader on the Senate Act.[2] The apology followed upon a threat to withdraw press privileges in the House from that paper. Had the article infringed the dignity of the House in a manner constituting contempt, legal action might have been taken by the House. As it happened, the threat of administrative action—the withdrawal of press privileges—struck at the news-gathering activities of the paper and produced the apology.

When newspapers published reports of 'Freedom Radio', a broadcast station operating in contravention of the Radio Act, a Minister took it upon himself to hint that their action might be construed as aiding and abetting the offender. There followed an immediate discontinuance of these reports.

In the professional field the Bar has always produced doughty defenders of civil liberty both in the courts and in the political field. Today few advocates will be found who would advise any member of the Bar with any pretensions to advancement in this profession and its ultimate goal of judicial office, to give expression to criticism of government policies. It is better to remain silent whatever one's views might be.

Enough has been said to enable the reader himself to answer the claim mentioned earlier in this chapter that the government has it in its power to silence opposition if it is so minded. The

[1] The then Minister of Economic Affairs a few years ago, when referring to the political movement known as 'the Natal Stand' and the possible support that it might receive in Durban, unfortunately coupled that subject with a reference to Durban's merchants and import permits.

[2] An Act which increased the number of members of the Senate and thus enabled the government to secure the two-thirds majority necessary to remove the coloured voters in the Cape from the common roll.

more important question, whether it has silenced criticism within the Union, is also now capable of answer.

It has not done so completely, though the inroads in the extra-parliamentary field are substantial and perilous enough. So long as the press remains free of censorship the voice of protest will still have a medium open to it. But the fences of restriction are being drawn closer and the area of freedom is every year becoming more and more circumscribed. The trend indicated in the report of the Commission of Undesirable Publications is a clear signpost pointing that way. That legal avenues and media of expression continue to remain open, however, is not enough if intimidation and fear of the sanctions of administrative disapproval so rule his mind that the subject will no longer take the risk of using even these media.

Jennings says: 'An opponent of a *dictator* is an *enemy* of the State.'[1] Should South Africa not beware lest by treating the opponents of government policies as enemies against the security of the State, it does not itself incur the odium of the corollary implicit in this statement?

---

[1] *The Law and the Constitution* (3rd ed.), p. 260. The italics are ours.

CHAPTER VII

Economic Freedom

While an increasing proportion of the African population is to be found in the cities and towns, most of the African male workers are actually domiciled in the Reserves, from which they go out to seek remunerative employment. A small number must be considered as having acquired urban domicile. The present policy of the Union is to limit the acquiring of urban domicile as much as possible. It is accepted policy, for example, not to allow any more Africans to acquire freehold ownership of land in the urban areas. A series of Urban Areas Acts, stretching from 1923 to 1957, limits and controls the African town-dweller—one and all based on the principle that in general he must be regarded as a temporary visitor to the place where he works, a migrant labourer in an area really foreign to him. Since nearly all industries are obviously urban, this means that the African worker, though vital to industry, is regarded as a temporary sojourner within it, and there is a reluctance to give him the rights usually given to workers in these days. This conception is a fundamental one and will repay study before we go further.

The declared policy of the government is to stimulate the economic progress of the Reserves—a policy which is surely good, so far as it goes—and to facilitate the establishment of as many industries as possible on the borders of the Reserves and drawing their labour force from them. No informed person feels that this in itself will mean the disappearance of Africans as workers from the great industrial centres such as Johannesburg or Durban. Such a policy, unless accompanied by the wholesale introduction of white immigrants as artisans and labourers (which is not South African government policy) would spell economic ruin to the Union. To go into the future with an admitted need for the permanent employment of hundreds of thousands of Africans in the towns and cities, and yet to treat the actual workers in virtually every case as temporary visitors from the country, is surely neither equitable nor permanently practicable.

Migrant labour, though a long-established institution in the Union and often not unacceptable to the Africans themselves, is satisfactory neither from an economic nor from a social point of view. Economically it means an abnormally high turnover of labour, with a consequent loss of experience and skill. Thus the monthly turnover of labour in a large Durban factory over a five-year period varied from 3·1 per cent to 12·3 per cent.[1] Socially it means that family life in the Reserves suffers disastrously. It upsets the traditional distribution of work.

Huts fall into disrepair, ploughing is delayed, and crops do not get proper attention. Normal bonds between husband and wife are more often than not broken. Immorality is common, and illegitimacy both in the Reserves and in the towns tends to increase. The husband, in the absence of normal family life sets up some sort of home with another woman in the city or tends to lead a loose sexual life. The woman in the Reserves seeks relations with other men in the area. . . .

Migrancy has brought about serious problems for the health administrator. The spread of diseases such as tuberculosis, venereal diseases and typhoid, is a direct result of the movement of people between the Reserves and the towns.[2]

Is migrant labour really necessary? Can the Reserves feed themselves? A recent research[3] on the Natal Reserves has shown that while the minimum maize requirements for a normal diet for 957,000 Africans in the Natal Reserves were 149,292,000 lb., the actual production of these areas in two recent years was 78,416,000 lb. and 97,628,000 lb., respectively. 'The serious food shortages, which money incomes do not adequately supplement, can hardly have any other results than the precarious existence and the low state of health of most of the inhabitants of the Reserves.'[3]

This is not the place to examine all the implications of the policy of apartheid, but it may be said without fear of contra-

---

[1] *The African Factory Worker* (Report No. 2, Durban Economic Research Committee, Oxford University Press, Cape Town, 1950), Appendix V.

[2] Brookes and Hurwitz, *The Native Reserves of Natal* (Vol. VII, Natal Regional Survey, O.U.P., Cape Town, 1957), pp. 86–7.

[3] Brookes and Hurwitz, op. cit, p. 129.

diction that neither the apartheid policy recommended by the Tomlinson Commission on the socio-economic conditions of the Native Reserves nor the somewhat diluted version of this accepted by the Union government will be able to dispense with African labour in urban areas. Whether this is regarded as permanent or 'temporary', for all the foreseeable future there will be a large movement of labour from the Reserves to the areas of employment outside them, and this movement is very stringently controlled by the Urban Areas Acts, which we shall now have to study.

Coloured and Indian labour is, on the whole, not migrant labour, and great as are the disabilities of coloured and Indian workers they are at any rate not subjected to the restrictions of the Urban Areas legislation.

The first Natives (Urban Areas) Act was passed in 1923. After numerous amendments, a consolidated Act went through Parliament in 1945. It was promptly amended in the same session of Parliament and amending Acts were passed in 1946, 1947, 1952, 1953, 1955, 1956, and 1957. With all this mass of amending legislation a trained lawyer can only keep in touch by assiduous study, yet any breach of the law may lead to legal proceedings against, and in a large number of instances to the summary arrest of, the ignorant tribal African who comes into the urban areas to seek work.

The first point to grasp is that no African can come freely to an urban area and seek to find work for himself. The reasons for this, in great measure, are the desire to avoid serious unemployment and housing problems in the urban areas; but the protection of agriculture by diverting labour to farms is also an important reason. However good or bad the motives may be, the fact remains that the African does not have freedom of movement in his own country, nor freedom to seek for work where he desires it. The essential point of this legislation is that 'no native shall remain for more than seventy-two hours in an urban area'[1] without special permission, except in the case of the wife, unmarried daughter or minor son of an African exempted from this provision.

Exemption is granted to any African born and continuously[2] resident in the area, or any African

[1] Act 54 of 1952, sec. 27.   [2] Act 36 of 1957, sec. 30.

who has worked continuously in such area for one employer for a period of not less than ten years or has lawfully resided in such area for a period of not less than fifteen years, and has thereafter continued to reside in such area and is not employed outside such area and has not during either period or thereafter been sentenced to a fine exceeding fifty pounds or to imprisonment for a period exceeding six months.[1]

Since it is impossible to tell by looking at an African whether he has been in the area for more or less than seventy-two hours, the law must either be a dead letter or must be enforced by the police stopping Africans and questioning them. It is perhaps an inevitable consequence of this system that

in any criminal proceedings against a native in respect of a contravention of the provisions of this section, it shall be presumed until the contrary is proved that such native remained in the area in question for a period longer than seventy-two hours.[2]

An African entering an urban area for a bona fide visit must, therefore, take a chance of being arrested, or, if he wishes to avoid this, must spend hours at a crowded and congested Native commissioner's office to establish the fact that he had entered the town as a bona fide visitor that day. Moreover, he is liable to arrest on his way from the railway station to the Native commissioner's office, that is, while actually doing the only thing that he can do to establish his bona fides: this is not a mere hypothetical case, for instances of police questioning in these circumstances are personally known to us. The penalty for any offence under this section is, for the first offence, a fine not exceeding £10 or imprisonment not exceeding two months or both such fine and such imprisonment; in the case of a second or subsequent offence, the maximum fine is £25 and the maximum period of imprisonment three months.[3]

It seems incredible that any law in any civilized country can submit a man to arrest and imprisonment while he is actually on his way to a public office to comply with the law; and if it be argued that such provisions are necessary to counteract widespread evasions of the law, surely this constitutes a severe condemnation of the whole system.

[1] Act 36 of 1957, sec. 30.   [2] Act 54 of 1952, sec. 27(4).
[3] Act 25 of 1945, sec. 44.

If the entrant is a bona fide work-seeker, he must report before the expiry of the seventy-two hours to an authorized officer.[1] That officer may give or refuse him permission to seek for work. If he refuses him, he usually names a date after which he cannot legally be in town, and endorses this on the document which he carries. But he cannot give permission unless the African concerned has been permitted to seek work by a labour bureau at his home magistracy. Many cases are known to us personally of Africans who have been sent back— in some cases hundreds of miles, involving the expense of a double rail-journey—to get this permission.

The labour bureaux, which are offices of the Native Affairs Department, cannot compel an African to take up any specified job, but they can, in certain circumstances, remove alternative opportunities from him. In particular, they can refuse him permission to enter an urban area, and at the same time indicate to him that a job is available as a farm labourer, and this they frequently do. The African may refuse, but he must then forgo the chance of paid labour unless he is lucky enough to find a paid job other than farming in his own area. The procedure of refusing permission to enter an urban area and at the same time indicating farm employment is a common one. It is not 'forced labour' but it is perilously near it. Farm labour is necessary, and under a good employer the worker may find it healthy and attractive, but can one justify even the indirect use of compulsion to divert to it a man who does not want it but prefers urban employment?

It is permissible, when leave is granted to seek work in an urban area, for the local authority to stipulate the *class of work* for which the permit is granted. Thus the African can be restricted in his very search for employment to seeking a particular class only.[2]

Such a system, while generally not abused in the manner indicated below, certainly lends itself to abuse. It is shocking to think that so much depends on the good faith and incorruptibility of minor officials. The following illustration from life, reported in the *Rand Daily Mail* on 14 August 1956, is very striking:

---

[1] Act 25 of 1945, sec. 23(1)(b).
[2] Act 16 of 1955, sec. 5(b); see *Annual Survey of South African Law*, 1955, p. 308

An African, arrested for a minor trespassing offence when he took a short cut, was brought before a court and sentenced to £4 or 40 days' imprisonment. He could not pay the fine. After a few days in prison he was sent to a farm fifty miles from Johannesburg. There, he alleged, he was forced to pick mealies from sunrise to sunset, with not even water to drink all day and only a ten-minute break at 3 p.m. to eat what he could carry in his hands of a dish of mealie porridge and potatoes. He was beaten daily by African foremen, and returned (this was testified to by the District Surgeon) with septic cuts on his arms, hip and back, a head injury and festering ankles, caused, he said, by blows and by chafing from the rough sack he was compelled to wear and by the heavy 200 lb.-size sack that was strapped to him in order that the mealies he picked might be put into it. At night he was locked in a concrete room with between fifty and sixty others, with but one bucket for sanitation, no washing facilities, and one tin of water each for drinking. No time was allowed in the mornings for cleansing these quarters. The men slept on dirty sacks, and three shared one blanket—this in the middle of winter. On return home this man was immediately admitted to hospital. The *Rand Daily Mail* traced another man who had been sent to the same farm and who gave much the same story.

The Native Affairs Department issued a Press statement on 15th August to the effect that thorough investigations would be made. The European farmer was subsequently exonerated, but eight African 'boss-boys' were charged with assault.

The registering officer, even if all other documents are in order, may refuse to issue a permit to seek work 'whenever there is a surplus of native labour available within the proclaimed area', and in a large number of other cases.[1]

Since, when an African has lost a job, it does not follow that he automatically gets permission to look for another one, immense power is put into the employer's hands, because dismissal from a particular job may, and sometimes does, involve expulsion from the urban area.

Complicated though this summary may seem, it is simple compared with the complexity of the laws themselves. The Non-European Affairs Department of the city of Johannesburg in a circular letter entitled 'Hints to Employers, Actual or Intending, of Native Labour', dated 14 December 1955—a

[1] Regulations under Government Notice 1032 of 1 May 1949, secs. 3 and 4.

document which is not critical of the system but purely factual
—states:

The engagement and discharge of Native labour has become a very
complicated matter *as there are so many rules and regulations concerning
Natives in general.* It is an important social duty for employers to
take care to provide fully and accurately the information for which
they are asked. Failure to do this and to obey all the instructions
given to them leads to endless difficulty, confusion and embarrassment for other employers, Natives and officials.[1]

To illustrate further the kind of difficulties involved, it may
be said that if an African has a permit to seek work expiring on
the 15th, and he finds an employer willing to engage him on
the 16th, the employer must first send him back to the registering officer to obtain a permit to seek work.[2] An African
residing on a farm may be allowed to seek work in town by
terminating his services on the farm, and then (if he is lucky
enough to do so) obtaining permission from his rural District
Labour Bureau to go to an urban area, and on arrival applying
for permission to seek work (his District Labour Bureau cannot
give him this); or alternatively he may come into the urban
area with the farmer's permission, but may be employed only
up to the date signified by the farmer as the date on which he
must resume work on the farm.

Even this is a simplification of the law, which differs somewhat as between farm labourers, farm-labour tenants, and
'squatters', but as the latter categories will fairly rapidly
disappear in terms of the provisions of Act 18 of 1954, we need
not labour the point.[3]

It will be noticed that in all this part of his life the African
is almost entirely in the hands of officials, government and
municipal, possessed of very wide discretion. An appeal to the
courts is possible in some cases, but often impossible.

Leaving this labyrinth of laws and regulations for a time,
we may go on to consider the more purely economic question:
what work may a non-European do?

The field of work open to non-Europeans is limited by law
and also by custom. Leaving the professions on one side, one

[1] Para. 15. The italics are ours.
[2] Para. 3(ii) of the 'Hints to Employers'.
[3] For 'squatters' see *Annual Survey of South African Law*, 1954, p. 302.

may say that employment on farms and in domestic service in urban areas presents no economic difficulties, though of course all the rigours and complexities of the Urban Areas legislation apply to the latter. Employment on the mines is regulated by special legislation (the Native Labour Regulation Act of 1911 and subsequent amendments). Great care is taken by the mining industry, the gold-mines in particular, to protect their employees and to arrange matters with the government departments concerned, so as to prevent friction and unnecessary arrests. The gold-mines are model employers so far as the housing, feeding, and health services for their employees are concerned; but the system of migrant labour and the wage structure of the industry are open to much controversy. In 1954 the mines and quarries of the Union employed some 450,000 Africans, over 2,500 coloured men and just under 500 Indians, as against some 62,000 Europeans.[1]

By custom, subsequently reinforced by law,[2] the higher posts in the mining industry are reserved for white, and in a very few instances for coloured, men.

In the nature of the case the greatest fields of employment left to non-Europeans, apart from the farms, the mines, and domestic service, are in commerce, manufacturing industry, building, and transport. In the building trade special legislative restrictions have been placed on the use of African building workers. Apart from this, employment in general is governed by restrictions, at first mainly customary, but coming more and more to be legislative, the general effect of which may be summed up, in simple language and without including a host of details, as follows:

(1) Restrictions on apprenticeship which effectively debar most non-Europeans and all Africans from becoming apprentices.

(2) Interference with the freedom of the trade union movement, such as to discourage and sometimes to prohibit, interracial trade unions, and virtually to destroy African trade unions altogether.

---

[1] Muriel Horrell, *South Africa's Non-White Workers* (S.A.I.R.R., 1956), p. 65.

[2] Notably the Mines and Works Act of 1911 and the Mines and Works Amendment Act of 1926.

(3) Exclusion of non-Europeans, partly by custom and partly by law, from the higher posts in industry, in particular from any posts where they may exercise authority over Europeans.

(4) Exclusion of Africans from the normal machinery for industrial conciliation, while none the less making striking a criminal offence.

We shall endeavour to examine this pattern in greater detail.

The legislation affecting the use of Africans in the building industry is to be found in Act 27 of 1951, as amended by Acts 38 of 1953 and 60 of 1955.

Section 15 of the Act[1] lays down, baldly enough, that 'no person shall in an urban area, elsewhere than in a native area,[2] employ any native on skilled work'.

'Skilled work' is defined in the principal Act at great length, and includes bricklaying, masonry, plastering, carpentry and joinery, painting, plumbing, electrical fitting and wiring, and also 'any other building trade or branch of such trade which the Minister may, by notice in the *Gazette*, declare to be skilled work for the purposes of the Act'.[3] When the Act was being debated in Parliament, the Minister frankly agreed with the Opposition contention that a white employer using his own African employee to whitewash his own garage would be contravening the Act.

As a kind of compensation for these restrictions,

the Governor-General may, on the recommendation of the Minister, made after consultation with the board, by proclamation in the *Gazette*, prohibit persons other than natives or any specified classes of such persons, from performing any specified class of skilled work in the building industry, within any native areas, except with the written consent of the Minister.[4]

This power has not been very widely used, and the restrictions the other way are not strictly applied against African jobbers and handymen working for private householders, but the Act effectually prevents building contractors from ever using Africans in skilled work.

[1] Act 27 of 1951, sec. 15, as replaced by Act 60 of 1955, sec. 2.
[2] Defined so as to include the residential areas (locations, villages, etc.) set aside for residence by Africans within the urban area.
[3] Act 27 of 1951, sec. 1(xvi)(1).   [4] Ib., sec. 16(1).

Apart from the building trade, the exclusion of non-Europeans (not only Africans) from any higher posts in industry has been until recently very largely customary. Almost plenary powers were conferred on the government by the Mines and Works Amendment Act of 1926, but these were not used to any extent outside the mining industry. Indirect methods were preferred, such as the dismissal of non-European labourers on the nationalized railways in favour of 'civilized' (that is, white) labour, or the refusal of the benefit of tariff protection to industries which did not employ a stated proportion of white labour. But in the year 1956 was passed a new and comprehensive Industrial Conciliation Act,[1] in terms of which the Minister is empowered[2] to prescribe 'the reservation . . . of work or any specified class of work . . . for persons of a specified race or for persons belonging to a specified class of such persons'. In terms of this law, the Minister of Labour, late in 1957, attempted to reserve for Europeans a large section of employment in the clothing industry, hitherto carried out mainly by non-Europeans,[3] and although he had to make some awkward retractions and withdrawals, the main principle of reservation is still held *in terrorem* over thousands of non-European workers.

The wide discretion allowed to the Minister in a matter affecting the livelihood of vast numbers of people is extraordinary. The Act is so worded as to exclude any possibility of an effective appeal to the courts. The Minister may direct an inquiry 'whenever it appears to the Minister that measures should be taken'.[4] The Minister may make a determination 'if . . . he deems it expedient to do so'.[5] The right of a man—and of course in practice it is the right of a non-European—to use his skill to earn a living depends on the absolute and uncontrolled discretion of the Minister. So the economic opportunities open to the numerical majority of the workers of South Africa depend entirely on the changing policies of political officers.

When the non-European has secured his job, such as it is,

---

[1] Act 28 of 1956.
[2] For full details see sec. 77.
[3] Up to approximately 80 per cent.
[4] Act 28 of 1956, sec. 77(1).
[5] Ib., sec. 77(7).

what about his pay?[1] Ever since the passing of the Wage Act
of 1925, the principle has prevailed that in the fixation of
wage rates there shall be no discrimination on the ground of
race or colour, and the considerable amendments introduced
in 1937[2] do not affect this fundamental principle. There are
some exceptions (for example, employment in Native Reserves)
but the main pattern is as indicated. The effect of this provision is that the employers—the great majority of whom are
Europeans—will not risk social disapproval and the displeasure
of the State by employing non-Europeans in skilled posts, when
the only selfish incentive to doing so—the cutting of the wage
bill—is missing. There may be much to say for the principle
'the rate for the job', if it is applied universally, but the three
greatest fields of employment for Africans—the farms, the
mines, and domestic service—are expressly excluded from the
provisions of the Wage Act. So is government employment!
So, since the passing of the Native Building Workers Act of
1951, is the building industry. Thousands of Africans have
benefited by the activities of the Wage Board, though it is
questionable whether even so they have been paid enough to
meet the rising cost of living, but the great bulk of the African,
Indian, and coloured workers are fighting a desperate battle
to maintain decent standards of life on the wages they get. A
very careful survey of the cost of living for Africans in the
locations and African townships in and around Johannesburg,
made as recently as 1954, shows that the monthly income of an
average African family of husband, wife, and three children
is £15 18s. 11d., and the bare minimum of expenditure
£22 13s. 7d., leaving a monthly deficit of £6 14s. 8d.[3] This
gap is met by various means, all of them productive of social
evils—economizing on essential food, piling up debts, blind-
alley occupations for children who should not be working at
all, and 'illegal' earnings, such as liquor selling and prostitution.
The figures have varied, but essentially this sort of thing has

[1] A word might here be inserted about the professions. In form the non-
European is freer here than in the trades, but in practice the African advocate
can expect few briefs except from an African attorney, and the would-be African
attorney can generally not find a European to article him. The operation of the
Group Areas Act also stultifies their efforts to earn a living as private practitioners.

[2] Act 44 of 1937.

[3] Olive Gibson, *The Cost of Living for Africans* (S.A.I.R.R.).

been said with truth for some three decades, and the evil still persists. In few countries in the world is there so big a gap as in South Africa between skilled and unskilled wage rates, and the fact that wage determinations have no colour bar matters very little when we recollect that the great bulk of the skilled workers are Europeans, and all but a negligible proportion of the unskilled workers non-European.

In these circumstances much would depend in a free country, basing its life on a free economy, upon the ability of the workers to organize themselves for collective bargaining, and upon the nature of the machinery provided for industrial conciliation. To these topics we shall now address ourselves.

The trade union movement among white workers has existed from the days before the formation of the Union of South Africa. Gradually, coloured, Indian, and later African workers became members of trade unions. Before 1948 'mixed' trade unions and coloured and Indian trade unions were all recognized. African trade unions were never accorded legal recognition, though some measure of *de facto* recognition was coming to be accorded to them by the Department of Labour in the years immediately before 1948. The trend of State policy in the past decade has been to hinder in every possible way the formation of 'mixed' unions, to refuse any recognition *de jure* or *de facto* to African unions, and to provide alternative measures for dealing with labour disputes affecting Africans—measures in which no place was provided for African unions.

African trade unionism has never been a flourishing concern in South Africa, and this is not surprising, if one bears in mind that most of the workers concerned are migrant labourers, the majority of whom still have roots in the Reserves. The story of the rise and fall of the one 'general' union—the Industrial and Commercial Workers' Union (I.C.U.)—is too long and too irrelevant to our present subject to be told here. Its success and failure were much bound up with the genuis and limitations of its founder and leader, Mr. Clements Kadalie. When the I.C.U. faded away, the foundation of individual trade unions was undertaken, and had a brief period of limited success.[1]

[1] For these facts about the African trade union movement we are indebted to the chapter 'Trade Unions' in the *Handbook on Race Relations in South Africa*, published for the S.A.I.R.R. (O.U.P., Cape Town, 1949).

When the movement reached its peak in 1944, there were sixty-five African unions in the Transvaal, the only province where the movement reached significant proportions. In 1947 there were only half a dozen such unions in good financial standing. The policy of separate African unions has thus not led to impressive results, yet legislation has effectively barred the entrance of Africans into the ordinary trade unions of the country.

Some of the organizers of these unions were communists, and some have suffered under the Suppression of Communism Act. In all fairness it should be said that these enthusiastic young Marxists were doing work which few other white men were able and willing to do. On the other hand there is always the feeling that communist enthusiasts seek *ultimately* (as orthodox teaching bids them to do) the well-being of the party and of the revolutionary programme for which it stands. Finance has been the Achilles' heel of most African political and economic organizations, and the trade unions have suffered from the Africans' failure to pay their dues, a failure the more intelligible when one remembers that African trade unions are not only unrecognized but also treated with hostility. In recent years the exclusion of all Africans from the machinery of the Industrial Conciliation Act[1] has weakened still further the chances for African trade unionism, and its influence is today negligible.

The best way to teach African workers the principles of trade unionism and to educate them in the methods and technique of successful collective bargaining would be to include them as ordinary members, or as members of recognized affiliated branches, of the accepted trade unions. This, as we shall show, is now forbidden by law, but while it was still possible the white trade union movement was slow to act, itself in many cases maintaining a colour bar. It may seem strange to those well read in the history of industrial organization in other countries that the workers should perpetuate divisions among themselves, and so be unable to approach the employers with a united front, but political and emotional considerations have often prevailed over economic arguments in the history of modern South Africa. Until quite recent times

[1] By Act 48 of 1953, sec. 36.

the bulk of the labour movement in South Africa has been a
white labour movement, and, now that so many Afrikaans-
speaking Nationalists are employed as miners and industrial
workers, the fervour of nationalism is added to existing colour
prejudice. Few indeed are those Afrikaans-speaking miners
and factory workers who are workers before they are
Nationalists.

The Industrial Conciliation Act of 1956 (No. 28 of 1956)
aims at recasting the trade union system on the basis of apartheid. African workers having been already excluded (by Act 48
of 1953) from the regular industrial conciliation machinery,
their unions having been refused recognition, and alternative
machinery having been devised for settling their disputes, it is
perhaps not surprising that 'employee' is defined as 'any
person (other than a native) employed by or working for any
employer'.[1] The Act therefore, excluding the African, deals
with the respective positions of white persons, coloured persons,
and Indians in the trade union movement. Its provisions may
thus be summarized as follows:[2]

(i) *No further 'mixed' unions to be registered*

The Act provides that no further 'mixed' trade unions—
that is, unions providing for both white and coloured membership—will be registered.[3] Special exemption may be granted by
the Minister in cases where the number of white or coloured
workers concerned is so small that they could not form an
effective separate union.

(ii) *Creation of machinery for possible splitting of existing unions along racial lines*

Existing mixed unions are then dealt with. The Minister of
Labour said during the debate that there were forty-four trade
unions registered for whites only, nine for coloured workers, and
one for Asiatics.[4] Also, there were 125 registered for both white
and coloured, although in fact members might be from one of
these groups only. The Act provides that should over half of

[1] Act 28 of 1956, sec. 1(1)(xi).
[2] This summary is taken, with permission, from the *Survey of Race Relations*,
1955–6 (S.A.I.R.R.), p. 176–8.
[3] Sec. 4(6).
[4] Assembly, 23 January 1956, *Hansard* 2, col. 268.

the white or of the coloured members of an existing mixed
trade union, in the industry and area for which it is registered,
wish to break away and establish a separate union along racial
lines, they may apply to the Industrial Registrar for registration. Appeal from his decision lies to the Minister of Labour,
and thereafter, if desired, to the courts of law.[1]

The position might, then, arise in which over half of the
white members of an existing mixed union seceded, leaving a
minority of whites in the original body. It is stated in the Act
that in such cases the Industrial Registrar, after consultation
with the original mixed union, may vary the terms of its registration to exclude all white members. Similarly, if over half of
the coloured members of an existing mixed union should break
away, membership of the original body may be confined to
whites only. Again, appeal lies to the Minister and thereafter
to the courts of law. As members of the Opposition pointed out
in Parliament, the closed-shop principle on a racial basis may
thus be introduced.[2]

It was previously possible for a trade union to split along
racial lines (provided that there was no closed-shop provision
in the industry and area for which the union concerned was
registered), but those seceding forfeited any share of the funds
of the original body. The new Act alters this position. It provides
that up to one breakaway white union and one new coloured
union may obtain a share of the assets of the original mixed
union, provided that they have among their membership
workers who in the five years preceding the commencement of
the Act were members of the mixed union during the currency
of a closed-shop agreement (that is, persons who were forced
to belong to the mixed union).[3]

Wherever possible, the unions concerned are to find a basis
for the division of the assets, but if no agreement has been
reached within twelve months of the breakaway, the matter
must be referred to the Industrial Registrar. He is empowered,
if he wishes, to consult a public accountant or actuary. After
then giving the unions concerned the opportunity of submitting
representations, he will make an order relating to the division

[1] Secs. 4(3), 7(2), and 16(1).
[2] Assembly, 13 February, *Hansard* 5, col. 1515.
[3] Sec. 6.

of assets. Should good cause be shown, he may later vary the provision of or withdraw such an order. An appeal lies, not to the ordinary courts of law, but to an industrial tribunal to be established in terms of the Act. A ruling by this tribunal will have all the effects of a civil judgment. There is no further appeal to the Appellate Division on questions of fact, only on points of law.

(iii) *Any remaining 'mixed' unions to create separate branches for white and non-white members*

It is also provided that from twelve months after the Act came into operation (7 May 1957) any mixed trade unions which continue to exist must have separate branches and hold separate meetings for their white and coloured members.[1] Again, the Minister may grant exemption in cases where there are so few white or so few coloured members that a separate branch could not function effectively; but such exemption may at any time be withdrawn.

A new provision was added by the select committee and subsequently adopted by Parliament: that the executive committees of remaining mixed unions must consist of white persons only, unless the Minister grants special exemption. Except for these office-bearers, no member shall attend a meeting of a branch other than his own; nor shall a coloured person attend a meeting of the executive committee except at this body's request, for the purpose of interrogation or of reporting, or in order to carry out his functions as an official.

These provisions will strike most unprejudiced critics as being humiliating towards the non-European worker; but the point must not be lost sight of that the freedom of the white worker to organize with maximum effect for the protection of his rights is directly hindered by this legislation, as is his right to associate with whom he will in his capacity as a worker. He is virtually compelled to be segregated, whether he wishes it or not.

The machinery which the Parliament of South Africa has set up for the Africans as a substitute for trade union organization is to be studied in the Native Labour (Settlement of Disputes) Act of 1953, No. 48 of 1953. Briefly summarized,

[1] Sec. 8(3).

7

the Act sets up a Central Native Labour Board and regional Native labour committees, to act as the equivalents of industrial councils or industrial conciliation boards. It is specifically provided that every member of the board shall be a European.[1] The regional committees, however, consist of Africans under the chairmanship of a European official, designated a 'Native Labour Officer'.[2] Works committees may be elected by African workers in any establishment where there are not less than twenty such workers, and one member of the committee may be appointed as a 'liaison member' to keep in touch with the regional committee.[3]

Strikes and lock-outs are absolutely prohibited under penalty of a fine not exceeding £500 or imprisonment for a period not exceeding three years or such imprisonment without the option of a fine or both such fine and such imprisonment.[4] A like penalty rests on any persons who incite, or express sympathy with or lend support to, a strike or lock-out.

Striking has been a criminal offence so far as Africans are concerned, and 'pass-bearing Natives', that is, all but a small minority of the African workers, were excluded from the original Industrial Conciliation Act of 1924. Recent legislation has, therefore, not departed sharply in principle from the pre-1948 situation; but it has eliminated exceptions, tightened up the rules, and made the penalties more harsh. The position may be summed up by saying that the African as a labourer, no less than as an urban resident, is treated essentially as a temporary migrant, is kept wholly apart from general trade union organization, and is provided with a paternalistic protection under the domination of white officials as a substitute for learning the hard lesson of self-help, while any drastic action such as a strike is a criminal offence, resulting in severe penalties.

When the African worker is in town, he cannot live where he likes. If he is not housed in 'compounds'—this is the system used by the gold-mines and many other large-scale employers of African labour—he must reside in a location, village, or hostel (the latter a sort of municipal compound for men

---

[1] Act 48 of 1953, sec. 3(2).   [2] Ib., secs. 4 and 8.
[3] Ib., sec. 7.
[4] Act 59 of 1955, sec. 1, substituting a new sec. 18 in Act 48 of 1953.

without families) approved by the Native Affairs Department under the provisions of the Natives (Urban Areas) Consolidation Act of 1945. The Act also makes provision for other areas set aside for African residence, but such relatively 'free' areas are rapidly diminishing. It is the declared policy of the present government not to allow Africans to acquire freehold rights in urban areas. Locations, villages, and hostels are controlled by white superintendents administering the numerous regulations under the Urban Areas Act.

This chapter is an attempt to survey the economic position of South Africans, especially those of African race, in so far as they affect civil liberties, and it is out of the question to embark upon an exhaustive study of the general economic position. It is essential, however, to refer to the long-continued and very grave housing shortage for African workers. Each of the two world wars resulted in marked industrial development in the cities of South Africa, African labour streamed in to take up jobs often in industries essential to the war effort, and neither industrialists nor the municipalities succeeded in housing their workers adequately: some hardly tried. As a result, in all large industrial centres—and especially around Cape Town and Johannesburg—Africans had to fend for themselves. They were not allowed to acquire land, and there was no land upon which they could legally build shanties or huts for themselves. They therefore broke the law—as they had to if they were to do the work they had been asked to do—either by living in back rooms let to them by rack-renting landlords, or by irregularly occupying land (often, though not always, paying rent—sometimes a high rent—for it) and building on it hovels of various types. It is noteworthy that the interiors of these appalling dwellings were often neat and clean, with suitable furniture. This process of building a collection of hovels on an unauthorized site is known as 'squatting'. To meet the situation, the government and municipalities have in some instances stepped in, set aside an authorized site, supplied services such as water and sanitation, and encouraged Africans to build their own shanties. This process is often termed 'controlled squatting'.

By Act 52 of 1951, uncontrolled squatting is made an offence, the penalty prescribed being a fine not exceeding £25 or imprisonment for a period not exceeding three months or both such fine and such imprisonment. The court may also issue an order for summary ejectment. Although the Act makes provision for the establishment of emergency camps ('controlled squatting'),[1] there is no assurance that emergency or other provision must be made for workers before they are ejected from their irregular homes, fined or sent to goal, with their homes demolished; and cases have occurred where workers were prosecuted without any alternative legal accommodation being made available to them, and where their only recourse, if they were to remain in the urban area and continue to earn, was to build another wretched hut on another irregular site and hope for the best.

Coloured and Indian housing was at one time mainly an economic problem—the problem of dealing with low-paid workers living in slum conditions. The whole question is now complicated, even for the well-to-do minority,[2] by the provisions of the Group Areas Act and its numerous amending (but not ameliorating) Acts. These have been dealt with in Chapter II.

A system of contributory unemployment insurance was introduced for all races in 1946,[3] but their benefit was later deliberately removed from African workers.

All workers enjoy the benefits of the Workmen's Compensation legislation, but at descending levels depending upon race.

Before concluding this chapter, it is necessary to refer to the question of government employment. The opportunities of such employment for non-Europeans are, in general, very limited. A few higher-paid posts are available for them in the

[1] Act 52 of 1951, sec. 6.

[2] There is a widespread but very mistaken impression that Indians in South Africa as a whole are well-to-do. Recent research on Indian incomes (C. A. Woods, *The Indian Community of Natal*, Vol. IX, Natal Regional Survey, O.U.P., Cape Town, 1954) shows that out of an earning force of some 53,000 Indians in the Transvaal and Natal, more than 30,000 were earning less than £100 per annum and an additional 16,000 did not reach the £200 level. In the principal towns of the Union the average wage earned was £176 per person per annum, in the rural areas £113 per person per annum. The few rich men—and less than 1·2% of the earning force draw more than £1,000 per annum—are particularly hard hit by the restrictions of the Group Areas Acts, and in some areas, particularly in Pretoria, the capital of the Union, the congestion in Indian housing is appalling.

[3] Generally by Act 53 of 1946; previous partial systems had been created by legislation in 1937 and 1942.

Native Affairs Department, the post office, and (in increasing numbers) in the police. Most, where employed at all, are employed in the lowest-paid jobs, for example, as cleaners or messengers. None are appointed to the top ranks of the public service and no non-European is ever placed by the State in a position of authority over Europeans. A special barrier has been raised during the last three decades against the employment of Indians by the State. For example, between 500 and 600 Indians were employed by the South African Railways in 1954, as against 1,800 in 1924. Some 1,850 Indians are employed by the Durban Municipality in 1954, as against over 4,000 in 1937–8.[1] (Of course members of all races are employed as teachers in government schools for their own particular race groups.)

The economic life of the Indians has been systematically attacked by government legislation and administration. Except for isolated cases among coloured people and Africans, they are the only non-European group that has produced capitalists and employers of labour. These have been harassed by governments of both political parties, and Europeans of both races, and petty commercial jealousy has joined hands with nationalistic theory in hindering and thwarting them; but this process has never been so devastating as it has been during the last seven years, that is, since the passing of the Group Areas Act. The coloured people, too, who once provided the artisans and skilled craftsmen of the Cape Peninsula, have lost ground. While the main impact of restrictive legislation falls on the African worker, the disabilities of the other non-European groups must not be forgotten.

[1] C. A. Woods, *The Indian Community of Natal* (Natal Regional Survey, Vol. IX).

CHAPTER VIII

Educational Freedom

The greater part of this chapter must be devoted to the direct attacks made by legislation on educational freedom—the Bantu Education Act, which has limited fundamentally the freedom of education among the Africans and was avowedly meant to do so, and the Separate Universities Bill, which set out to impose very stringent limitations of liberty in university education, especially as regards non-Europeans.

Before dealing with these attacks, however, it is necessary to refer to the present position of European education, and the significance of the educational ideals of the powerful Christelike Nasionale Onderwys (Christian National Education) movement, especially as this movement is very influential among the majority of members in three of the four provincial councils, which control European school education. In one province (the Transvaal) these ideals have been carried into effect, mainly by administrative action on the part of that provincial education department, more thoroughly than elsewhere.

The minimum conditions of educational freedom in any country are that the State, while maintaining its own schools in adequate numbers, should not interfere with the existence of reputable private schools (confessional or otherwise); and that the parent should have a free choice as to the kind of school to which he sends his child. Up to the present, the former of these conditions has been fully observed so far as European (and indeed non-African) schools in three of the four provinces are concerned, although there have been occasional threats of interference. The second condition has not been observed, yet the reasons for non-observance are extremely plausible and may be felt by some to be reasonable.

The measure of parental coercion that exists is bound up with the question of the medium of instruction. In one province only (Natal) is it left to the parent to decide whether his child shall go to a school where the teaching is given in the English language or to one where Afrikaans is used as the medium. In the other three provinces, the final choice rests with the Administrator on the recommendation of the school inspector, and the policy is to educate every child through the medium of the language most commonly used in the home, although it is complained that the tests given by principals and inspectors seek to find out with which language the child is most familiar, not that most commonly used in the home. The educational arguments for this policy, if of course it is fairly applied, are strong. The school should be linked with the home and not form an artificial world, and the child will learn more rapidly and thoroughly if he is taught in the language with which he is most familiar. None the less, there are many who feel that the parent ought, on principle, to be free to decide this issue for himself.

There is a deeper reason for the strong objections raised by some. While English-speaking parents have a reasonable choice of sending their children to schools, governmental or private, which will leave them free to think for themselves or at any rate not indoctrinate them with theories which are repugnant to the beliefs of the home, it is claimed that many Afrikaans-speaking parents are, in three provinces, denied this choice. There is only a very small number of private schools that employ the Afrikaans language as medium. Thus the insistence on the use of the home language as medium means that almost every Afrikaans-speaking child must go to a government school. Rightly or wrongly, it is claimed that Afrikaans-medium government schools are impregnated with the ideals of 'Christelike Nasionale Onderwys', and that teachers who diverge strongly from these ideals need not look for promotion. Thus, an Afrikaans-speaking supporter of the United Party (and *a fortiori* an Afrikaans-speaking 'liberal') is placed in the position that he is compelled to send his child to a school where he is in danger of being indoctrinated in the views of his parents' political opponents, for the connexion between the philosophy of the Christelike Nasionale Onderwys movement and that of the Nationalist Party is felt to be an intimate one.

We believe these views to be substantially correct, but of course some of them may be contested. If they are correct, it undoubtedly follows that the educational freedom of a substantial minority of Afrikaans-speaking parents is seriously curtailed.

One way of escape is open to the Afrikaans-speaking parent who is wealthy enough to avail himself of it. Since ordinary school education is controlled by the province, he may send his child to an English-medium school in a province which permits this. This is done in some instances, but it relieves the situation in only a small proportion of the cases affected. It is obvious that if all education were taken over by the Union, and if the Union Parliament were to legislate (as it almost certainly would) in favour of compulsory mother-tongue education, this safety-valve would be closed.

In the province of the Transvaal the 'home language' principle is applied even in the case of private schools, subsidized or unsubsidized, and by the Transvaal Education Ordinance of 1953 the Transvaal Provincial Administration is given wide powers of control over curricula and staff appointments in private schools. At the time of writing, these powers have not been taken by the provincial authorities of the Cape and the Orange Free State, and there seems little danger of their being taken in the foreseeable future by the provincial authorities of Natal, but, as has been suggested above, if the Union took over all education from the provinces, Natal could be coerced.

There is a difference of opinion among observers as to the general policy of the Christelike Nasionale Onderwys movement and the Nationalist Party with regard to English-medium schools, governmental or private. Some hold the view that these may hope to enjoy a somewhat contemptuous toleration, provided that the English-speaking group continues to form a permanent and slowly dwindling political minority, and there has been much in the absence of direct interference in the past to bear out this view. Others feel that these recent attacks on the educational freedom of English-medium schools in the Transvaal are fair warning of a policy which may become general. In government schools there are ways and means of exercising indirect control, especially if it becomes clear that amenability on the part of the teacher is the highroad to promotion. Even now, few government schools, even in Natal, would dare to take any action which was in conflict with the principle of apartheid. There are not wanting voices to warn

South Africans that even the influential and famous private
schools of the country may be attacked, and this, though it
would inflame English-speaking public opinion to a dangerous
pitch and therefore possibly be rejected as politically unwise,
cannot be dismissed as a mere chimera after the sharp and very
successful attack on African private schools. As Professor
Michael Roberts, formerly of Rhodes University, Grahamstown, said in 1952, 'Christian National Education professes
(disingenuously, I think) to be concerned only with schools for
Afrikaans-speakers; but it is essentially at English schools that
this latest blow[1] is aimed', and he goes on to protest with great
justification at the continual trend towards control and
uniformity. At any rate, on one point, the attitude towards
apartheid, it would seem that those now in authority will be
strongly tempted to take powers to ensure uniformity and
orthodoxy.

What are the ideals of the Institute for Christian National
Education? As outlined in a document officially issued by it
in 1948, they involve indoctrination both religiously and
politically.

By Christian instruction and education for Afrikaans-speaking
children we mean instruction and education given in the light of
God's revelation in the Bible as expressed in the Articles of Faith in
the three Afrikaans Churches. (Article 2.)
By national instruction and education we mean instruction and
education in which adequate expression is given in the whole content of instruction and in all the activities of the school to the
national principle of love for one's own, based on and within the
terms of the Christian principle, so that the child is introduced to
the spiritual-cultural importance, the spiritual-cultural wealth, of
the nation, and becomes a worthy bearer of that cultural wealth.
(Article 3.)

The document proceeds to define the place in education of the
home, the Church, the State, and the school. In these definitions, given with some elevation of language, there is much
that can be read with sympathy and respect. Nevertheless,
there are disquieting statements such as that the Church 'must
exercise disciplinary measures, when the need arises, with

[1] i.e. the Transvaal Provincial Ordinance of 1953, at that time published in
draft form.

reference to the doctrinal opinions and lives of the teachers as members of the Church' (Article 8[4]), and that training colleges for teachers should 'function as Christian and National institutions' (Article 9). In technical colleges the teachers should be 'Protestant Christians and bilingual South Africans' (Article 12[7]). Instruction in civics should be 'such that it will produce Christian and national citizens' (Article 6[4]). In practice Christian National Education tends to make belief in apartheid a matter of Christian and national faith, and to give nationalism in general almost a mystical religious aura.

The views of the Institute of Christian National Education on the education of Africans are of very special importance as they form essentially the basis of the Eiselen Commission's Report on Native Education (1949–51), which in turn forms the basis of the Bantu Education Act of 1953. It seems right, in all fairness, to give the relevant Article 15 of the Institute's statement of principles, unaltered and unabridged, so as to avoid all possibility of misrepresentation:

We believe that the vocation and task of white South Africa with respect to the native is to christianize him and to help him on culturally, and that this vocation and task has already found its immediate application in the principles of trusteeship, not placing of the native on a level with the white, and in segregation. For this reason we believe that any system of teaching and educating natives should be based on these principles. In accordance with these principles we believe that the teaching and education of the native must be based on the Europeans' attitude to life and to the world, more particularly that of the Boer nation as the senior European trustee of the native; and that the native should be led, *mutatis mutandis*, to an acceptance of the Christian and National principles in education as these principles are more fully described in Articles 1, 2 and 3, provided it be an independent acceptance. We believe also that the mother-tongue is the basis of native instruction and education, but that the two official languages of the country should be learned as subjects, because they are official languages of the country and constitute for the native the keys to that adoption of culture which is necessary for his own cultural advancement. Because of the cultural immaturity of the native we believe that it is the duty and task of the State in co-operation with the Christian Protestant Churches to provide and superintend education for natives. We believe however that the actual teaching and education of natives and the training of native teachers should be undertaken by the natives themselves as soon as possible, but under the control and guidance of the State; with the proviso that the financing of native education be placed on such a basis that it is not provided at the cost of European education. Finally we believe that instruction and education for natives must lead to the development of a native community on Christian-National lines which is self-supporting and provides for itself in all ways.

The Report of the Eiselen Commission on Bantu Education (1949–51) is, if one may say so without offence, far less naïve in setting out its principles than the terms of Article 15 quoted above, but essentially it goes in the same direction. 'Bantu education', it says (paragraph 777), 'does have a separate existence, just as, for example, French education, Chinese education or even European education in South Africa, because it exists and can function only in and for a particular social setting, namely, Bantu society.' And its whole tenor is in the direction of maintaining the tribal system and perpetuating tribal and linguistic differences, for example, by limiting entrance into high schools to one language group and one only. Throughout it looks on education as a part of socio-economic development and assumes that this must be on the basis of apartheid. The best commentary on the Report is, however, the Bantu Education Act, which has been throughout in the hands of the Chairman of the Commission, Dr. Eiselen.

The fundamental provision of the Bantu Education Act[1] is to be found in section 9, which prescribes that all Bantu schools, existing or still to be brought into being, must be registered, that registration may be refused in the absolute discretion of the Minister of Native Affairs, and that *the maintenance of any unregistered Bantu school is an offence, punishable by fine or imprisonment.*[2] Apart from the effect on schools existing at the passing of the Act, the fact remains that no school for Africans may now be opened, however reputable, however independent of

[1] No. 47 of 1953.
[2] It may be objected that this power existed previously under various provincial ordinances; but it was almost completely dormant. As far as we have been able to ascertain, it was used on very rare occasions to prevent undesirable denominational competition, never once because the province disliked a school or disagreed with its teaching; and such activities as vacation courses or night schools did not in fact have to apply for registration.

government subsidies, unless the Minister of Native Affairs approves of it; and it has become very clear that he will not permanently approve of any school which runs counter to the policies of the Institute of Christian National Education and the Eiselen Report. It is not the refusal of subsidy which is the difficulty, but the fact that one cannot open a school without making oneself subject to criminal proceedings, and this is surely a very marked curtailment of civil liberty.

Under this law, registration has been refused to some large, very reputable, and very successful schools, which have had to close down. One of them was over 100 years old. In other cases church authorities have been allowed to continue to conduct the hostels but (as in the case of the world-famous Lovedale) have been extruded from the school itself. Everywhere the new philosophy of education is making itself felt. In general the African cannot feel that he is being educated for freedom in a free state; he is being educated to fit into a pattern which, whatever merits it may have in other respects, rests on colour discrimination as a fundamental principle.

The *general* effect of the Act after some five years of operation has been to put the conduct of Bantu schools increasingly in the hands of men chosen by the Native Affairs Department to carry out its own policy of education as defined in the Eiselen Report, and by the application of disciplinary measures to silence African teachers who would like to criticize the Act or the Department's policies of education, or to offer unacceptable alternative views.

In this respect the 'regulations governing the conditions of appointment, service and discipline of Bantu teachers in Government Bantu schools', published under Government Notice No. 841 of 22 April 1955, call for study. The definition of 'misconduct' in Regulation 16 is such as to apply to any teacher who

(h) encourages through his acts or behaviour disobedience or resistance to the laws of the State;

(i) identifies himself actively with a political party, or body, or actively participates in political affairs;

. . .

(l) contributes to the press by interview or in any other manner, or otherwise publishes a letter or article criticizing his superior officers or the policy of the Department of Native Affairs; or

(m) behaves or acts or neglects to act in a manner which in the opinion of the Secretary is deleterious to his position as a teacher, regardless of whether such behaviour, act or negligence has been defined in these regulations or not.

It is to be observed that in the omnibus clause (m) the words 'in the opinion of the Secretary' cut out virtually all appeal to the courts, and that in terms of clause (l) any public criticisms of the policy of the Department of Native Affairs becomes an offence. The force of this becomes clearer when one recollects that the Department of Native Affairs is today concerned with almost any aspect of African life, and that teachers are, through their education, among the most obvious leaders of thought among their people.

Misconduct under these heads may lead to dismissal.[1] Legal representation is denied to any accused teacher at a disciplinary inquiry[2] (a European teacher is entitled to representation under the appropriate provincial ordinances). The decision of the Secretary for Native Affairs on the case is explicitly declared to be final.[3]

Early in 1957 there was introduced into Parliament a Separate University Education Bill. It provided for the exclusion of African students from the 'open' universities (Cape Town and the Witwatersrand), and also from the University of Natal, where they had always been taught in segregated classes; for the separation of the purely non-European medical school from the University of Natal, and of the University College of Fort Hare from Rhodes University, with which it had been affiliated; and for the establishment of separate 'Bantu' (African) university colleges and separate university colleges for other non-European groups. The separate university colleges for Africans were to be placed under the Department of Native Affairs, not the Department of Education, Arts, and Science, which has hitherto been the Department responsible for all university education. The University of South Africa (at present purely an examining body for external students) was to be responsible for the examinations at these segregated institutions.

[1] Regulation 15(f).   [2] Regulation 19(5).
[3] Regulation 20(3).

Since the Bill affected institutions like the University of Natal and the University College of Fort Hare, which were already segregated, many of its critics urge that the government, in introducing a measure so full of restricting clauses, is concerned with the control of university teaching as well as with racial segregation.

During the parliamentary session of 1957 the point was raised that the provisions relating to the Natal Medical School and to Fort Hare affected private interests, and that the Bill was therefore a 'hybrid bill'; and as the procedure laid down for 'hybrid bills' had not been followed, the Bill was withdrawn from the Order Paper and a new Bill, excluding these two bodies from its scope, was introduced. This passed its second reading in the House of Assembly and was referred to a select committee which should report to the 1958 session of Parliament. Whether the Bill will be carried in 1958 and what final form it will take remains to be seen.

It is to be noted at the time of writing we are dealing with a *Bill*, not an Act of Parliament, and one which may possibly not be enacted. The danger of its becoming definitive law is, however, so great, and its provisions so significant that it seems necessary to discuss it.[1]

The effect on the existing universities is regarded as very serious. While the Bill does not interfere with 'academic freedom' in the narrower sense in these institutions, it most certainly interferes with the broader interpretation of university independence by refusing the universities the right to decide who their own students are to be, and that on the irrational and non-academic criterion of race. Moreover, by placing, as we shall show, restrictions on 'academic freedom' even in the narrower sense on the new segregated university colleges, it provides a precedent which university teachers feel to be dangerous and which they cannot feel confident will not be applied in future to the older universities.

[1] When Parliament rose in 1957, the select committee became a commission. In August 1958 the report of this commission, which included a minority report, was published and an amended Bill, called the Extension of Universities Education Bill, was introduced into Parliament. While the Bill differed in certain minor respects from the original, it retained most of the objectionable features which are discussed in this chapter. The Bill was withdrawn, owing to pressure on parliamentary time, and will, according to present information, be introduced in 1959.

What are the restrictions on the new 'segregated' university colleges referred to above?

The Minister[1] may establish or disestablish any such college. Its council shall consist of 'not less than three members to be appointed by the Governor-General', one of whom the Governor-General is to designate as chairman, in contra-distinction to the practice in the older universities, on the councils of which government nominees are in a minority. The senate is to consist of the principal, and 'such other members as the Minister may from time to time appoint', while the senates of the older universities, membership of which is defined by statute, consist mainly of all the professors in the university. The principal is to be appointed, not as in other universities by the council in consultation with the senate, but by the omnicompetent Minister. The appointment of members of the teaching staff rests with the Minister, who may also discharge any member of the teaching staff for misconduct, defined under seventeen heads, which include the following:

(a) public adverse comment upon the administration of any department of the Government or of any province or of the territory of South West Africa; and . . .

(g) the propagation of any idea or taking part in or identifying himself with any propaganda or activity or acting in a manner calculated—

(i) to cause or promote antagonism amongst any section of the population of the Union against any other section of the population of the Union,[2] or

(ii) to impede, obstruct or undermine the activities of any Government department.

In these unusual university institutions, it is the Minister again who may limit the number of students permitted to register for any course, or who may refuse admission to any student applicant 'if he considers it to be in the interests of the university college concerned to do so'. It is the Minister again who may determine at which place a student shall attend for the purpose of receiving instruction. The Minister may make

[1] So far as the three segregated African institutions are concerned, this will be the Minister of Native Affairs, not the Minister of Education, Arts, and Science.

[2] This is similar to the offence under the Riotous Assemblies Act, yet dismissal is not made dependent upon a conviction for an offence under that Act, but on the *authority's opinion* that the offence is committed.

regulations as to the discharge of students, as well as to many other matters, such as, for example, the constitution and functions of boards and faculties. He may delegate any or all of his functions to the Secretary or to any other senior official in his Department, but apparently not to the council or senate of the university college. In effect we have here a case of complete and unrestricted control by the executive government of something strikingly inappropriate to such control — university education.

Let us now see the extent to which the freedom of African education has disappeared or is in the process of disappearing. The African child can go to no school of which the Minister of Native Affairs does not approve, and while it is not fair to say that this means he must attend a school which is run on the lines indicated in the principles of the Christelike Nasionale Onderwys movement and quoted earlier, it is quite safe to say that he will never have the chance of attending for long any school which challenges those principles. Up to matriculation he must attend a school intended for members of his own 'ethnic group' and in the earlier years the language of that group will be his medium of instruction. If the Separate University Education Bill is passed in its present form, he will, if permitted to do so by the Minister of Native Affairs, attend one of the separate university colleges for Africans—whichever one the Minister directs him to—and choose a university curriculum among the faculties and departments permitted by the Minister, under a principal and academic staff appointed by the Minister and dismissible by him. It is fairly safe to prophesy that few men will apply for, and fewer still will retain, these curious academic posts unless they are either supporters of the Minister or time-servers. Not here will the African student breathe the fresh air of free university life, and —always so long as the Bill is passed in its present form—he will not be permitted to attend any other South African university. If at this stage or as a post-graduate student he wishes to study abroad, he will have to obtain a passport from the Minister of the Interior, who as a matter of routine refers all African passport applications to the Minister of Native Affairs; and passports may be refused at the absolute discretion of the Minister.

Here is the perfect example of the absence of all educational freedom, of regulation by political and administrative authorities, without any appeal, of all education from the infant class to the Ph.D.

So far as other non-Europeans (Indians and coloured) are concerned, the position is a little, but only a little, better. If the Separate University Education Bill goes through, they too will be confined to university colleges of the type indicated above, with all the same restrictions, with the single alleviation that the controlling Minister and Department will be Education, Arts, and Science, rather than Native Affairs, and that therefore purely educational considerations may presumably sometimes weigh more heavily, and political ones less so, than in the case of Africans. Passports for overseas education will be in the unfettered discretion of the Minister of the Interior.

At the present moment, however, Indian and coloured children attending primary and high schools are under the supervision of the several provinces, of which at least one and probably not more than two are not committed to the views of the Christelike Nasionale Onderwys movement, and of which all still permit missionary and other non-governmental schools to function. It is impossible to say how long those schools will be left under the provinces: their future is uncertain.

The European child is in a better position, yet if he is Afrikaans-speaking he will be compelled in three of the four provinces to attend an Afrikaans-medium school, which in general will either be guided by or at least not violently hostile to the principles of Christelike Nasionale Onderwys, and the Afrikaans-speaking parent who has different views has no way out unless he can afford to send his child to a private school in another province. In many of the universities there is a large measure of academic freedom, and in some of them views openly and strongly opposed to the orthodox government views on education and on colour are expressed without penalty.[1] If, however, the Separate University Education Bill

[1] But not without interference. It has, for example, been publicly stated that the Special Branch of the C.I.D. paid a student at Rhodes University, Grahamstown, to spy on his lecturers and fellow-students, and this is not the only interference of its kind. Moreover, recent proceedings against a lecturer in English at Stellenbosch University on the ground of the alleged *content* of his teaching have been very disquieting.

becomes law in its present form,[1] European university students will have to go abroad to meet non-white students, and will be deprived, in their most formative years, of discussing problems of common interest with their fellow students of a different colour. Thus, on a vital question the universities will be cut off from the reality of living in South Africa, and to that extent maimed in what should be the abundant life of their youth.

[1] See footnote on p. 117. It is worth repeating here that, though the new Bill has been through the process of a select committee and a commission, it does not differ materially from the old Bill, despite strong adverse criticism from Government-supporting academies.

CHAPTER IX

Religious Freedom

In general, religious freedom is very fully and fairly granted in South Africa, and that in spite of many difficulties not found in all countries which might give the State plausible pretexts for interference. In the sense that churches, within the widest limits set elsewhere, may worship as they please and teach whatever specifically religious doctrines they want to teach, religious freedom is pretty complete in South Africa, and any statement to the contrary is misleading. During recent years, however, religious freedom has been indirectly but very really limited, firstly, by the operation of the Group Areas Act and the Natives (Urban Areas) Act, leaving churches erected for members of one group unusable or almost unusable when the area in which they stand has been allocated to another group; secondly, by making the occupation of churches for Africans, whether in or out of Native areas, increasingly dependent on the unfettered discretion of the Minister of Native Affairs; thirdly, by making words said in church which might 'encourage or tend to encourage deterioration' in the relationship between Africans and governmental bodies a valid reason for cancelling the grant of a church site; and finally (1957) by giving the Minister of Native Affairs the right to intervene in order to prevent the attendance of Africans at church services together with Europeans. It will be observed that it is mainly the Minister of Native Affairs to whom these immense powers have been entrusted, and that they very specially affect churches for Africans: thus once again liberties which have been maintained on the broadest lines for many years are challenged when they come into conflict with the principle of apartheid.

Reference has been made above to 'many difficulties not found in all countries which might give the State plausible pretexts for interference'. One of these is the vast and constantly increasing number of African separatist churches. This proliferation of sects is amazing. To give reliable numbers at any given moment is impossible, for new ones are always springing up. In 1933 there were over 300, in 1945 about 800, in 1947 over 900, and recently it has been publicly stated that they number more than 1,000. They include the African Seventh Church of God Laodicean Mission, the Bible Standard Church of America, the Christian Catholic Apostolic Holy Spirit Church in Zion, the Ethiopia Church Lamentation of South Africa, the First Catholic Apostolic Church Jerusalem in Zion of South Africa, the Heaven Twelfth Apostle Church in Zion, the King of Salem Melchizedec Church, the New Progressive Baptist Church, the United Independent National Church of God, and the Zion Holy Church Nation of South Africa.

Some of the separatist churches (for example, the African Methodist Episcopal Church) have attained standards as regards membership, resources, and education of the ministry, which have won for them the respect of other churches and of officials. Some consist of a mere handful of men, led, for example, by an archbishop whose qualification is 'passed Standard 2', and of some, we fear, the words of Dr. Bengt Sundkler are only too true: they have become 'the bridge over which Africans are brought back to heathenism'.[1]

To give equal opportunity of acquiring sites to all these scores of sects in the limited area of a village is impossible. That all their ministers shall be given privileges such as concession facilities on the government railways could hardly be expected. Nor can the government recognize as marriage officers men of little or no education. A few of the separatist churches have been accorded full recognition, and perhaps the government has been a little too conservative in doing this, but no reasonable man could expect immediate and indiscriminate recognition of all. The practice is to require a recommendation from the permanent Native Affairs Commission, based largely on numbers of members and adherents, number of church buildings, financial position, and standard of education of the ministry. The discretion given is not always exercised in a truly judicial spirit, but we repeat that general recognition can

[1] *Bantu Prophets in South Africa*, p. 297.

hardly be expected. As far as can be ascertained, no church has ever been discriminated against on the ground of doctrine or ritual, and it is not usual to interfere with the holding of services or other activities, except in so far as church sites are concerned, on the part even of the 'non-recognized' churches.

There is another difficulty experienced in South Africa: it is the lack of unity among the recognized non-separatist churches. That the Roman Catholic Church finds it, as a matter of principle, impossible to co-operate regularly on religious matters with other Christian churches is not peculiar to South Africa; but the linguistic and ideological difficulties that keep the Dutch Reformed Church from joining in membership of the Christian Council of South Africa with the Anglican, Methodist, Presbyterian, Congregationalist, and other churches are a peculiarly South African phenomenon. Thus, on the most vital of issues in the religious field—the granting of power to the Minister of Native Affairs to prevent Africans from worshipping with Europeans—it was impossible to get joint action from the Dutch Reformed Church and the English-speaking churches.

In certain areas and among certain churches comity in the mission field has not always been attained and one denomination of Christians has left sectors of heathenism untouched in order to build a church close to and in competition with another Christian denomination. In these circumstances the State has had to step in, much as, when Turkey ruled Palestine, Musselman guards were used to keep the peace between Greek and Latin Christians. So in the Reserves the Native Affairs Department has had to see to it that a prescribed mileage intervenes between a church of one persuasion and a church of another. This has reinforced the natural claim of the Department to allocate church sites in the Reserves according to its discretion.

In the same way the municipal authorities, under the supervision of the Native Affairs Department, allocate a limited number of church sites in municipal locations and villages. In view of the facts set out above, it will readily be understood that they cannot satisfy every claimant, but, however natural and defensible their position may be, it must be remembered that it is impossible for a denomination excluded from the agreed sites to purchase a site of its own within the village, for all is controlled by authority. If, now, legislation precludes the acquisition of sites for African churches in urban areas outside the location limits, it will be seen that, despite the acceptance of the general principle of religious freedom, a new denomination could be denied the right to build churches through the whole length and breadth of the Union, except indeed on the farms of friendly farmers for their labourers. Not for one moment do we suggest that any denomination has been thus consciously and systematically excluded, but the fact remains that the right to enjoy a place of worship is not in this respect a legal right, but depends on the benevolent discretion of the Minister of Native Affairs and the municipalities. Further if the location is distant from the urban areas, the Minister, by refusing permission for the building of special churches for Africans and by exercising (in conjunction with the local authority) his power to ban mixed worship, may virtually close the door to religious services of any kind for numbers of Africans, particularly domestic servants. If it be objected that he would not, the answer is that he could, and that it is undesirable to make the right to worship dependent upon the unfettered discretion of a secular Minister.

Let us see how these tendencies are mirrored in recent legislation.

Act 46 of 1937 amended the Urban Areas Acts of 1923 and 1930 by enacting:

As from the commencement of the Native Laws Amendment Act,[1] 1937, no person shall conduct, on premises situated within any urban area outside a location, native village, native hostel or area approved by the Minister for residence of natives in terms of paragraph (h) of subsection (2) any church, school or other institution or any place of entertainment which is not in existence at the commencement of the said Act, mainly for the benefit of natives, without the approval of the Minister given with the concurrence of the local authority concerned, which approval may with like concurrence be withdrawn.[2]

---

[1] This is a frequently recurring title for omnibus Acts amending several laws affecting Africans. Act 46 of 1937 was one of these. The notorious Act of 1957, discussed later, was only one of a series bearing the same name.
[2] Sec. 5(7).

The effect of this enactment is to give the Minister of Native Affairs an absolute veto on the erection of new churches for Africans in an urban area outside the locations or other 'Native areas' after the coming into effect of the Act on 1 January 1938, and this even if the local authority raises no objection. Thus, the Minister is in a position to prevent the building of any church by a denomination that has come into existence since 1937, to prevent the rebuilding of a dilapidated existing church, to prevent the building of a second church by any denomination that has one already, and to prevent the building of a new church to replace one that, by the operation of the Group Areas Act or by administrative action on the part of the Department of Native Affairs, has been rendered useless because its congregation has been moving away.

This section was re-enacted as section 9(7) of the Natives (Urban Areas) Consolidated Act of 1945.[1]

It is to be noted that the 1937 Act was sponsored by the United (fusion) Party under General Hertzog, and the 1945 Act by the United Party under General Smuts. This fact was used as a strong debating point by Nationalist supporters of the notorious Native Laws Amendment Bill of 1957, and they were so far right as to make some of the opponents of the latest interference with religious freedom reflect with some shame on the precedents created with no opposition from them in 1937 and 1945. An examination of the contents of the Bill of 1957 will show, however, that the argument was disingenuous, for the new Bill went very far beyond the precedents of 1937 and 1945.

Section 29(c) of the Native Laws Amendment Bill of 1957 was drafted to replace section 9(7) of the Natives (Urban Areas) Consolidation Act—itself identical with section 5(7) of Act 46 of 1937 quoted above—by the following new provision:

No church, school, hospital, club or other institution or place of entertainment which was not in existence on the first day of January 1938, to which a native is admitted or which is attended by a native, shall be conducted by any person on premises situated within any urban area outside a location, native village, native hostel or area approved by the Minister for residence of natives in terms of paragraph (h) of subsection (2) nor shall any meeting, assembly or

[1] No. 25 of 1945.

gathering to which a native is admitted or which is attended by a
native, be conducted or permitted by any person on such premises
without the approval of the Minister given with the concurrence
of the urban local authority concerned, which approval may be
given subject to such conditions as the Minister may deem fit and
may be withdrawn by him after consultation with the urban local
authority concerned, or if he is satisfied that any such condition
has not been observed.

The reaction of white South Africa to this piece of legislation
was immediate, widespread, and inspired by deep feeling; and
it was up to a point effective. A letter signed by the Anglican
Archbishop of Cape Town (the Most Reverend Dr. G. H. Clayton) and dated 6 March 1957—Dr. Clayton died suddenly on
7 March and this was his last act—says:

The Church cannot recognize the right of an official of the secular
government to determine whether or where a member of the
Church of any race . . . shall discharge his religious duty of participation in public worship or to give instructions to the minister of
any congregation as to whom he shall admit to membership of that
congregation.

Further, the Constitution of the Church of the Province of South
Africa provides for the synodical government of the Church. In
such synods, bishops, priests and laymen are represented without
distinction of race or colour. Clause 29(c) makes the holding of such
synods dependent upon the permission of the Minister of Native
Affairs.

We recognize the great gravity of disobedience to the law of the
land. We believe that obedience to secular authority, even in
matters about which we differ in opinion, is a command laid upon
us by God. But we are commanded to render unto Caesar the
things which be Caesar's, and to God the things that are God's.
There are therefore some matters which are God's and not Caesar's,
and we believe that the matters dealt with in clause 29(c) are among
them.

Similarly, a statement signed by the President of the Conference of the Methodist Church of South Africa, the Secretary
of Conference, and the eight chairmen of districts, 'the
appointed leaders of the Methodist Church of South Africa
representing over a million souls', protests against the Clause
and concludes:

We wish to emphasise that the Methodist people are a law-abiding people, but if this legislation places us in the position where we have to chose between obedience to the State and obedience to God, we reiterate that our choice is clear. 'We must obey God rather than men.'

The Baptist Union of South Africa wrote:

We cannot agree that access to worship should depend on the permission of any State authority. Freedom of worship has been won at the cost of great sacrifice, and Baptists were among the first to suffer for this cause. As a denomination we recognize the supreme lordship of Christ. Should the State demand from us that which we believe we owe in loyalty to God, we must then choose to 'obey God rather than men'.

The Congregational Union of South Africa, which itself set the example a few years ago of electing a man of colour as chairman of the whole Union of Congregational Churches, the Church of Scotland, the Religious Society of Friends, and many other denominations joined in protest against the law.

The Archbishops and Bishops of the Roman Catholic Church said, among other things:

We consider that the Bill . . . constitutes a claim by the State to regulate the worship and religious practice of the individual person and we cannot admit such a claim. . . . There are many Africans working in the urban areas who can only fulfil their obligation of worship by attending church in urban areas other than a Native area. . . . We are charged with the safeguarding and the spreading of the Spirit of Christ, Who came to save all men irrespective of colour. That Spirit brings men together rather than separates them. The policy of the Minister is in the direct contradiction of this Spirit and we declare our opposition to it.

To the Minister perhaps the most influential protest came from the Council of the Dutch Reformed Churches of South Africa. Alone among the larger denominations the Dutch Reformed Church acquiesced in the Minister's amendment of his original proposals, but these at least were unacceptable to it. In their interview with the Minister the official representatives of the Church laid down these four principles:

(1) The gospel of Jesus Christ emanates from God to all mankind and is subject to no human limitations.

(2) The task is laid on the Church of Christ, in obedience to the Head of the Church, to proclaim the Gospel throughout the world and to all peoples.

(3) The right to determine how, when and to whom the Gospel shall be proclaimed is exclusively in the competence of the Church.

(4) It is the duty of the State, as the servant of God, to allow freedom to the Church in the execution of its Divine calling and to respect the sovereignty of the Church in its own sphere.

Faced with this remarkable chorus of protest, the Minister withdrew the clause in its original form, and produced a radically amended clause, less objectionable in practice, but in the view of most of the Christian churches still very objectionable in principle. This amended clause the Dutch Reformed Church, however, was willing to accept: in this, as we have stated, it stood alone among the larger churches.

In its final form, the clause is to be found as section 29(d) of Act 36 of 1957. After subsection (a), which re-enacts the provisions of section 5(7) of Act 46 of 1937, it proceeds:

(b) The Minister may by notice in the *Gazette* direct that the attendance by natives at any church or other religious service or church function on premises situated within any urban area outside a native residential area shall cease from a date specified in that notice, if in his opinion —

(i) the presence of natives on such premises or in any area traversed by natives for the purpose of attending at such premises is causing a nuisance to residents in the vicinity of those premises or in such area; or

(ii) it is undesirable, having regard to the locality in which the premises are situated, that natives should be present on such premises in the numbers in which they ordinarily attend a service or function conducted thereat,

and any native who in contravention of a direction issued under this paragraph attends any church or other religious service or church function, shall be guilty of an offence and liable to the penalties prescribed by section forty-five:[1] Provided that no notice shall be issued under this paragraph except with the concurrence of the urban local authority concerned, and that the Minister shall,

---

[1] On first conviction a fine not exceeding £10 or in default of payment to imprisonment with or without hard labour for a period not exceeding two months, to both such fine and imprisonment or to such imprisonment without the option of a fine. For second or subsequent offences the fine is raised to £25 and the period of imprisonment to three months.

before he issues any such notice, advise the person who conducts the church or other religious service or church function of his intention to issue such notice and allow that person a reasonable time, which shall be stated in that advice, to make representations to him in regard to his proposed action; and provided further that in considering the imposition of a direction against the attendance by natives at any such service or function the Minister shall have due regard to the availability or otherwise of facilities for the holding of such service or function within a native residential area.

This is obviously very different from the original 'church clause' quoted earlier, and, hedged round as it is by various restrictive provisos, may never be put into practice. But it is too soon to say that the new clause was merely a face-saving device and became obsolescent the moment it was enacted. In any case the African has no longer a *right* to worship where he pleases, but only a privilege dependent upon the Minister's non-intervention. For these and similar reasons the protesting churches have continued to protest against the clause in its new form, and several have announced their intention to disobey any ban if enacted, and have exhorted their congregations to do likewise.

Before we pass on to our next point, it will not be out of place to dwell for a short time on the use in the Native Laws Amendment Act of the phrase 'to cause a nuisance'. The normal and proper approach to the existence of 'nuisance' in urban government is to allow the local authority to legislate for it in its by-laws and to prescribe for contravention of the by-laws. If I disturb my neighbour by an unreasonable use of my radio, I am prosecuted, and normally that is sufficient to compel me to desist. The local authority does not seek power to expel me from my home or to eject me from the place where I cause the nuisance. Similarly, a European religious sect which causes disturbance and noise through its religious rites would be prosecuted under the by-laws. Humanity and municipal government alike do not require that it should be *denied* the place where it worships.

The foregoing suggests that 'nuisance' in section 29(*d*) in relation to Africans is not intended to refer to any misconduct on the part of Africans, but purely the *existence* of black people on a particular site or in an area. It is the *presence* which is really the nuisance, not the conduct. There is, however, no evidence that the mere presence of non-Europeans in a church or passing through an area is so disturbing to neighbours that it cannot adequately be dealt with by the existing methods of local government. The national character of the legislation makes it clear that something more than mere 'nuisance' is the cause of Parliament's legislating for what is really a municipal matter. No large municipality has made representations to the Minister to take national action! The truth is that the cause is apartheid, which requires the government to separate white and black in every conceivable circumstance, even in the act of worship.

The new legislation seems also cowardly and harsh, in that it penalizes the African worshipper for a contravention, but not the European clergyman, as in the first Bill. The Minister thus avoids a clash with the Church, while still depriving the African and penalizing him.

We pass to another aspect of religious freedom. Totalitarian regimes, whether Communist or Nazi, have tended, when they tolerated the Church, to limit it to its purely 'religious' functions, that is, to worship.[1] Whenever the State begins to interfere with the Church's freedom, it tends to follow to a greater or a lesser extent the same line. While, therefore, South African legislation leaves the doctrine and ritual of every church free from interference, it is not surprising that steady inroads are being made on their other activities. We have already seen that it is a punishable offence for any church to conduct a school for Africans, even at its own cost, without the permission of the Minister of Native Affairs. The constant indirect but real interference with multiracial social activities (see Chapter X) hampers the churches in another important field. The operation of the Group Areas Act and of other restrictive legislation frequently leaves the churches with buildings and other assets on their hands, through the removal of the populations that they serve to other areas. The extensive and excellent buildings of the Anglican Church in Sophiatown, Johannes-

[1] As one of the chief charges of communists against the Church is that it concentrates the attention of its people on 'pie in the sky by and by', the limitations which prevent the Church from education, health, and social work seem lamentably inconsistent, to say the least.

burg, are the best known but by no means the only example of this.

Finally, there is the attempt to prevent the use of the pulpit for any comments on public affairs which may be repugnant to the feelings of the government of the day. The provisions of the Suppression of Communism Act can be applied to this as to most situations, but there is another and more insidious line which can be taken. In reply to a question in the House of Assembly on 25 August 1953, the Minister of Native Affairs said that in future mission societies and church bodies wishing to obtain sites in urban African townships for the erection of churches or to renew existing leases of such sites would be granted leases for periods coinciding with the unexpired periods of loans by which housing schemes in the area were erected or of leases to Africans of housing sites in the area; but in no case would a lease exceed thirty years.[1] Leases of church sites might be cancelled if any activities conducted on the sites were such as to encourage or tend to encourage deterioration in the relationship between Africans and governmental bodies or were aimed at defiance or breaches of the law. The common law regarding compensation would apply if a lease was terminated before the expiration of the period for which it was entered into; but no compensation would be payable for improvements if the site remained in the occupation of the lessee for the full period of the lease.

It is not an innovation for conditions to be laid down for the occupation of church sites: the allocation of such leases is governed by paragraph (f) of section 42 of the Natives (Urban Areas) Consolidation Act of 1945. But whereas in the past it was required of mission bodies that the sites should be used only for the purposes for which the lease was approved, now the Minister of Native Affairs has assumed power to cancel the lease if in his opinion anything is said or done on the site which is not conducive to good relations between Africans and governmental authorities.

[1] *Hansard*, No. 7 of 11th Parlt., Col. 2201.

CHAPTER X

Social Freedom

To a visitor landing in the Union for the first time, the separation of social amenities for non-whites from those for whites is the most obvious and startling difference from other countries. The fact that men of different colour cannot occupy the same railway-compartment for a journey of any length,[1] cannot dine at the same hotels, cannot even drink a cup of tea together at a tea-room, makes clear how seldom any effortless social intermingling can take place. There have been in the past exceptional areas or institutions where this intermingling has been relatively easy. We shall show how opportunities of this kind have in recent years been steadily and systematically reduced. Every man's home is still his home, though less inviolate than formerly, and in some homes men of a different colour are welcome, but these are few. For the rebel against social apartheid needs to have enough courage to face social disapproval, sometimes ostracism, and in these days the risk of attention from the Special Branch of the C.I.D.

Some of this separation is prescribed by law. Much of it is a matter of custom, but very deep-seated custom with its own strong sanctions. Changes in the law introducing new restrictions will be studied in this chapter, but it is important to notice also changes in custom. Not all of these have been in a restrictive direction. Churches, universities, and social welfare groups have consciously moved away from the old pattern and encouraged occasional intermingling. On the other hand the attitude of government and public authorities has changed markedly since the days when President Kruger lunched with a prominent Indian at Rustenburg, and the Free State government entertained Moshesh and his sons to dinner in Bloemfontein.

[1] On the Cape surburban lines, while there are coaches for 'Europeans only' there are also 'unreserved' coaches, occupied mainly by coloured persons but which Europeans may enter.

Reference has been made to the interference with institutions where social intermingling was easy and natural. One of the most striking cases of this kind is missionary schools and colleges. Even in these bodies, incredible though it may seem, social apartheid was not infrequently practised in the past. Many of them, however, did have a greater or lesser amount of social meeting. In the vast majority of cases the Bantu Education Act has brought this to an end. Where schools have been taken over by the government it has been frowned upon or totally suppressed, and some of the schools where it was most common have been closed down.

The Separate University Education Bill, if passed unaltered, will remove all opportunities of natural contact among university students.

In a few cities in the Union, inter-racial, or, as they have generally been called, international clubs have been set up. These are directly threatened by the Native Laws Amendment Act of 1957. The relevant provision[1] of this Act reads as follows:

Except with the approval of the Minister given with the concurrence of the urban local authority concerned, and subject to such conditions as the Minister may deem fit, which approval may at any time after consultation with the urban local authority concerned be withdrawn by the Minister, no person shall on premises situated within any urban area outside a native residential area, conduct any school, hospital, club or similar institution which is attended by a native or to which a native is admitted, other than a native attending in the capacity of an employee thereat, unless such school, hospital, club or institution was being so conducted on those premises at the date of commencement[2] of the Native Laws Amendment Act, 1937 (Act No. 46 of 1937), or if the number of natives attending or admitted to such school, hospital, club or institution at any time exceeds the number of natives who attended or were admitted to that school, hospital, club or institution immediately prior to the commencement of that Act, provided that this paragraph shall not apply with reference to the admission of a native to any hospital in the event of emergency.

In a further subsection, the Minister is given the power to prohibit by notice in the *Gazette* the attendance of Africans at 'any school, hospital, club or similar institution' where such

---

[1] Act 36 of 1957, sec. 29(d).   [2] i.e. 1 January 1938.

attendance constitutes 'a nuisance to residents in the vicinity', or where 'the club or other institution is conducted in a manner prejudicial to the public interest'. Yet another provision arms the Minister with similar powers with regard to 'any place of entertainment'.

These powers have up to the time of writing been used very sparingly, but every club now exists on sufferance, permission is most unlikely to be given for the opening of any new club, and no club can face success with equanimity since it may find itself accused of 'creating a nuisance', and, if a pre-1938 club, may, under the Native Laws Amendment Act, 1957, referred to above, lose its precarious immunity through an increase in its membership.[1]

While inter-racial social welfare organizations are not yet directly prohibited by law, sustained efforts are being made to reduce the number of these bodies and to discourage unofficial inter-racial contacts through them. It is the avowed policy of the Department of Native Affairs to eliminate intermingling in inter-racial societies of this kind, and the Departments of Social Welfare and of Education, Arts, and Science have used their powers of granting or withholding subsidies in order to discourage intermingling. A philharmonic society in one city, for example, a university dramatic society in another have been threatened with the withdrawal of subsidy if they allow non-Europeans to attend their performances.

In the nursing profession, equal participation of European and non-European nurses in the control of the profession has been prohibited by law. The Nursing Act (No. 69 of 1957) provides that the ordinary representatives on the Nursing Council of nurses and midwives must be elected by nurses and midwives 'who are white persons'.[2] One person may be elected to the Nursing Council by the 'advisory board for Coloured persons', and one by the 'advisory board for Natives'. Even these representatives must, however, be white persons.[3] Separate registers of white, coloured, and Native nurses are to be kept.[4] Similar provisions are made with regard to the

[1] See later in the chapter for the effect of the Group Areas Act on clubs.
[2] Act 69 of 1957, sec. 3(2).
[3] Act 69 of 1957, sec. 4(1)(c).
[4] Act 69 of 1957, secs. 12(2) and (4), 14(2) and 15(2).

South African Nursing Association.[1] Thus is separation com-
pulsorily introduced in a professional body of a specially
humanitarian character, and the chance of friendly contacts
between its white and non-white members materially reduced.

The law that prevents Europeans from entering Native areas
without permission means another set of restrictions on social
intermingling.[2] Under it, any multi-racial social functions can
be stopped if the Department of Native Affairs wishes to stop
them. It has been invoked to prevent a retired professor from
visiting an African home to learn Zulu, to hinder a botanist
from collecting specimens in a Reserve, to warn a missionary
that if he goes into the Reserve he must not have any meal with
an African family there. And although it is often administered
with more common sense than this, it is a powerful deterrent
to any considerable social intercourse in the so-called 'Native
areas'.

The Group Areas Act is one of the most important statutes
affecting social intermingling; but, though it can be most
effective in preventing regular and permanent intermingling
(for example, the residence of a non-European permanently in
a white household except as a domestic servant), it still by its
definition of 'occupation'[3] allows 'a bona fide visitor for a total
of not more than ninety days in any calendar year of any
person lawfully residing on the land or premises' exemption
from the restrictive provisions of the Act regarding occupation.
It is, however, a most sobering thought that only a simple
amendment to these provisions of the Group Areas Act is
needed to make it a punishable offence to entertain a non-
European in a European home or vice versa. That this fear is
not an imaginary one is shown by the terms of Proclamation
No. 333 of 1957, published in *Gazette Extraordinary* No. 5969 of
1 November 1957:

All provisions of the said Act relating to the occupation of land or
premises shall apply also with reference to any person who is at
any time in or upon any land or premises in a group area or in the
controlled area for the purpose of attending any public cinema or
partaking of any refreshments in a licensed restuarant, refreshment

---

[1] Act 69 of 1957, secs. 35 and 38.
[2] Act 18 of 1936, sec. 24(1), and see Regulation 45 issued under Government
Notice 494 of 1937.   [3] Act 77 of 1957, secs. 15(2)(*b*) and 23(2)(*b*).

or tea room or eating house or as a member of or guest in
any club, as if his presence constituted occupation of such land or
premises.

The effect of this Proclamation in any city where group areas
or specified areas have been proclaimed is that any person
attending any public cinema is deemed to be 'occupying' the
cinema, any person partaking of refreshments in a restaurant
is deemed to be 'occupying' the restaurant, and any person
attending any club as a member or guest is deemed to be
'occupying' the club premises. Unless a permit to the contrary
is issued, a non-European 'occupying' premises in a European
area (or vice versa) may be fined up to £220 or imprisoned
up to two years or may be subjected to both such fine and such
imprisonment.

It may be noted here that what may not be done under the
Native Laws Amendment Act may be done under the Group
Areas Act, which is, of course, a most far-reaching measure.

To sum up the situation, free, regular, and unembarrassed
social intercourse between white and non-white is discouraged
by the South African State. In some cases (for example,
establishment of inter-racial clubs) it is hindered by law, in
many cases it is hindered by administrative action, in almost
all cases it is visited with social disapproval. It may well be
regarded, and often is regarded, it would seem, by those
responsible for internal security, as prima facie evidence of
communist or other undesirable tendencies, rendering the
person concerned suspect. For example, the Special Security
Branch of the C.I.D. has been known to take the car registration numbers of people (including clergymen) attending a
mixed gathering in a private home. Such action may well be
regarded as intimidation.

The loss of natural and frequent contacts across the colour
line does immense harm. The practical result is to make contact in the main the prerogative of 'advanced' political parties
or associations or of earnest groups of slightly embarrassed
people meeting to discuss 'race relations'. In general, doctors
do not meet across the colour line to discuss questions of
medicine, photographers to discuss photography, philatelists to
exchange stamps, musicians to hear music.

The 'marginal' non-European, who is keenly interested in

such things, suffers thus a very great loss, and it is not only what he misses but also the positive harm done to him by the growth of bitterness, protectiveness, and isolation that needs to be taken into account. It may be added that the absence of contact in the professions seriously threatens the *standards* of professional conduct and skill. For instance, the relegation of an African advocate in Johannesburg to one of the local locations for his chambers cuts him off from the educative stream of daily contact with his profession, and from use of one of the greatest tools of that profession, namely, a good library.

But the white man too impoverishes himself by all this, and finds himself, by conforming to the social conventions of his time and place, assisting unwillingly, perhaps half-unconsciously, in supporting the apartheid policy. Freedom cannot thrive in an atmosphere so sultry and sullen, so heavy, so laden with the germs of separation and dislike and fear. To challenge this atmosphere demands courage, and in the circumstances of the case it tends to be done in a most frustrating atmosphere of unnatural good will, marred by the feeling that one is making a heroic stand; and this in a field of life where naturalness, unforced equality, and give-and-take, not without humour, are of the very essence of success.

CHAPTER XI

The Franchise

By the South Africa Act of 1909, the parliamentary franchise in the Union was declared to be, until the Union Parliament should itself prescribe the qualifications necessary to entitle persons to vote, the same as existed in the several colonies at the establishment of the Union.[1] Parliament was given a free hand to legislate on the franchise, except that no voter registered, nor who might become capable of being registered, in the province of the Cape of Good Hope might be disqualified by reason of his race or colour only, except by a Bill passed by a joint sitting of both Houses of Parliament and at the third reading agreed to by not less than two-thirds of the total number of members of both Houses.[2]

The qualification of voters in the four colonies at the time of Union, and therefore the original qualifications in the four provinces of the Union, were as follows:

In the Cape of Good Hope, there was no barrier of race or colour as regards the franchise. Any male person who had for twelve months occupied property to the value of £75, or who had for twelve months been in receipt of salary or wages at the rate of not less than £50[3] and who in addition could sign his name and write his address and occupation,[4] was entitled to be registered as a voter. Occupation of land or quit-rent tenure under the Glen Grey Act or similar Proclamations in the Transkei did not qualify the occupier for franchise,[5] but there was no restriction laid on Africans or other non-Europeans as such.

---

[1] 9 Edw. VII, c. 9, secs. 35–6.   [2] Ib., sec. 35.

[3] Cape of Good Hope Constitution Ordinance, 1852, sec. 8; Act 9 of 1892 (Cape), sec. 2.

[4] Act 9 of 1892 (Cape), sec. 6.

[5] Thus the paramount chief of a tribe might not be qualified as a voter since his income was not 'salary or wages' and his rights of occupation were on a quit-rent basis, while his paid secretary earning over £50 per annum might vote. This anomaly was preserved by the Representation of Natives Act, 1936, and still exists.

In Natal, Europeans or coloured persons were entitled to be
registered as voters if they were owners of immovable property
of the value of £50 or renters of such property to the yearly
value of £10,[1] or if they had an income of £96 per annum.[2]
Act 8 of 1896 enacted that persons 'who (not being of European
origin) are natives or descendants in the male line of natives of
countries which have not hitherto possessed elective representative institutions founded on the parliamentary franchise'
should be disqualified as electors unless they obtained an
exempting order from the Governor-in-Council. As far as can
be ascertained no exempting orders were ever issued.

The object of this legislation was to prevent Indians from
obtaining the franchise, and it succeeded in its aim. The rights
of persons already duly enrolled were not affected by the Act.
It appears that there was at least one Indian still on the
common voters' roll at the time of the passing of the Asiatic
Land Tenure and Indian Enfranchisement Act of 1946. Any
Indian so registered at the present time would have to be at
least 82 years old (21 in 1896); as far as is known there are
none so registered today.[3]

Ever since 1865 Africans in Natal were debarred from registration as voters unless they were exempted from the operation
of Native Law and possessed certain other qualifications. By
Law 2 of 1883 (Natal) they required, in addition to twelve
years' residence in Natal and seven years' exemption from
Native Law (which in itself required the support of three duly
qualified electors of European origin), a special letter of
exemption granted by the Governor. The form of application
for this exemption was required to be filled in personally by
the applicant in the presence of a magistrate or justice of the
peace, and the filling in was in fact a test of literacy and indeed
of some degree of education. The Governor was not required
to grant the letter of exemption, and usually did not do so.

The effect of this provision was to exclude Africans from the
franchise in Natal almost entirely. Not more than five ever

---

[1] Charter of Natal, 1856, sec. 11.
[2] Law 2 of 1883 (Natal), sec. 3.
[3] In any case they were, it would seem, removed from the common roll by
Act 28 of 1946, and not restored by the repealing Act, No. 47 of 1948.

held it at any one time, and only one was on the common voters' roll at the time of the passing of the Representation of Natives Act, 1936. He was allowed to remain on it until his death in 1945.

In the Transvaal and the Orange River Colony (Orange Free State) manhood suffrage for Europeans only was the rule, and no non-Europeans of any kind possessed the vote.

By Act 18 of 1930 all European women over the age of 21 were given the vote in all four provinces, without any property, income, or educational qualification. For a short time, therefore, there existed in South Africa the situation, surely unique in the world, where women held the vote on better terms than men. This anomaly was rectified by Act 41 of 1931, which introduced adult white franchise.

Therefore, in 1936 (the year of the passing of the Representation of Natives Act), the franchise position in the Union was as follows:

Subject, in all cases, to the usual disqualifications (for example, lunacy, sentence of imprisonment beyond a prescribed period), all European men or women over the age of 21 held the vote.

Coloured *men* only (not women) had the vote in the Cape and Natal if possessed of the qualifications mentioned earlier in this chapter (ownership, occupation or income, and education), which remained in force for them when no longer required for Europeans.

Indian *men* only (not women) had the vote in the Cape on the same terms as coloured men. In Natal those Indians who were on the voters' roll before 1896 and who continued to possess the general qualifications as applying to coloured people were also registered as voters. This body of electors consisted, of course, of a rapidly diminishing number of elderly men.

African *men* only (not women) had the vote in the Cape on the same terms as coloured men. In Natal they were still theoretically able to qualify for the franchise, but by 1936 only one African was on the roll.

Three points should be noted at this stage.

(1) No non-European woman has ever possessed the franchise, and none possesses it now.

(2) No non-European man or woman ever possessed the franchise in the Transvaal, and the Orange Free State, and none possesses it now.[1]

(3) Prior to 1936 such non-European voters as were registered were registered on a common voters' roll along with Europeans.

The important thing about the Representation of Natives Act (No. 12 of 1936) was that it took African voters in the Cape Province off the common roll and gave them the franchise on a separate community roll. Thenceforth they were represented not as citizens but as Africans. The qualifications remained the same as before (property of £75, or wages of £50 plus a slight educational qualification). No one was disfranchised. Any man reaching the age of 21 and possessing the other qualifications could qualify as a voter after 1936 no less than before it. But the voters were separated from the general electorate, and their representation was limited to three seats in the House of Assembly. This limitation, though it could of course be lifted by a subsequent parliament in the unlikely event of one being elected which was willing to do so, was a serious one. Exclusion from the common roll, look at it how we will, was something of a stigma, and meant a definite loss both of status and of influence. Finally, the fact that this reduced franchise was limited to the Cape Province and on the old Cape qualifications gave it the air of a survival of an old right preserved as an act of favour, not of a truly national non-European representation.

This national representation it was sought to provide by very different methods, namely:

(1) representation in the Senate;
(2) the bringing into being of a Natives Representative Council.

The provisions for the election of four senators to represent Africans are very complicated, but none the less the representation has been of some value, and as a supplement to Assembly representation might still be acceptable. It can, however, never

[1] Except that Indians in the Transvaal might be registered as voters on a very limited franchise under the Asiatic Land Tenure and Indian Representation Act along with Indians in Natal (No. 28 of 1946). This Act was later repealed by Act 47 of 1948 before any actual registration had taken place.

THE FRANCHISE 143

be a substitute for this, and that is what it is expected to be in Natal, the Transvaal, and the Orange Free State.

There are four electoral areas, each to be represented in the Senate by one senator:

(i) the Transkeian Territories;
(ii) the rest of the Cape Province;
(iii) Natal;
(iv) the Transvaal and the Orange Free State combined.

In the Transkeian Territories the election has hitherto been made by the African members of the United Transkeian Territories General Council. It will now be made by the Territorial Bantu Authority, which has replaced the Council.

In the other three areas the process of nomination and election is carried out by four types of 'voting units'. In the Reserves (scheduled Native areas) the voting units are:

(a) local councils—or in future, Bantu regional authorities as such are formed;
(b) chiefs, each voting on behalf of his tribe, in the large number of areas where no local councils or Bantu regional authorities exist.

Outside the scheduled areas, the urban inhabitants have as their voting units:

(c) municipal Native advisory boards existing under the provisions of the Urban Areas legislation;
and the rural inhabitants have:
(d) *ad hoc* electoral committees, chosen by specially summoned taxpayers in each of the wards into which the magisterial district has been divided.

Every voting unit has a numerical value obtained by determining the number of taxpayers under its jurisdiction. This numerical value varies considerably. Here are six concrete examples taken at random from a recent electoral list:

A municipal Native advisory board.	42
An electoral committee . . .	20,112
A local council . . .	21,966
Chief A	220
Chief B (a close neighbour of A)	13,463
Chief C	52

In a 'voting unit' containing several members, the decision of the majority determines the whole of the voting unit. Thus if six members of the local council instanced above voted for candidate X and three for candidate Y, X would poll 21,966 votes, not two-thirds of that figure.

A candidate, to be duly nominated, must secure the support of voting units to the numerical value of at least 2,000 votes and in addition must possess the qualifications of an elected senator under the South Africa Act (i.e. a South African citizen *of European descent*[1] at least 30 years old and the owner of landed property to the value of £500).

Should an election be necessary, the same procedure is followed. All returns are certified and sent in to the Chief Native Commissioner, who is the electoral officer for the area. In practice the nomination contest almost always eliminates all but two of the candidates, occasionally all but one. Candidates with little support fall away by refusing to accept nomination. Any campaigning begins well before, not after, the nomination date.

As chiefs are mostly illiterate they declare their vote verbally to the Native commissioner (magistrate). In theory this procedure has its dangers but hitherto there have been no disquieting reports of influence or intimidation, except in one unfortunate instance. More serious are the very inadequate checks on candidates. No election expenditure returns are called for and there is no limit to the expenditure which a candidate may incur. It is probable that bribes have been offered and accepted on occasion. Chiefs frequently consult their counsellors and influential friends and sometimes their people before casting their votes, and are considerably influenced by educated African leaders, who thus have a greater share in the conduct of elections than would appear from the letter of the law.

The whole system of representation is oddly at variance with the administrative set-up. The senator may well feel it his bounden duty to be in strong opposition to the government of the day, yet it is difficult for him to fulfil his parliamentary functions, and even to hold meetings, without some measure of

---

[1] The significance of this stipulation is discussed later in this chapter.

co-operation from the Department of Native Affairs, both at headquarters and in the districts. Chiefs, too, who are in one way government servants, are also electors who may choose a candidate very unacceptable to the government. The system would not have worked even as well as it has without considerable restraint on both sides, but as years pass by the representation tends to go a little more to the left, and the government a great deal more to the right than in 1936, and co-operation will probably prove increasingly difficult.

Ever since the first Union Parliament the Senate has contained four senators nominated by the Governor-General-in-Council 'on the ground mainly of their thorough acquaintance, by reason of their official experience or otherwise, with the reasonable wants and wishes of the coloured[1] races of South Africa'. This number was increased to eight by the Senate Act (No. 53 of 1955), to which may be added one nominated on similar grounds from the territory of South West Africa under Act 23 of 1949. With a few exceptions in earlier years of the Union, such senators are always supporters of the government which nominated them, and have no necessary contact with the non-Europeans whose interests they represent and no systematic meetings with them or their political organizations. Some never meet them, as senators, at all. While it would not be either just or seemly to say that this system has no value, it must be clear that it is in no real sense *representative*.

The Senate of 1936 consisted of forty-four members, of whom four (one-eleventh) were *elected* representatives of the Africans. The Senate as altered by the Senate Act of 1955 consists of eighty-nine members[2] but the representation of Africans has not increased proportionately and is now under one-twenty-second of the total. Moreover, the powers of the Senate have been reduced, since now it has only a suspensive veto, and cannot force a joint sitting in the case of repeated disagreement; and it is probably right to say that its prestige has fallen, even among those who supported the recent changes. Thus as the

[1] As printed in the Act 'coloured' (as distinguished from 'Coloured') means all men of colour, including Africans and Indians and is equivalent to 'non-European'.
[2] Ninety if we include the senator recently nominated under the Separate Representation of Voters Act.

years have gone by the value of this representation has been much diminished.

It should be mentioned that all parliamentary representation of the Africans in both the Senate and the House of Assembly is by Europeans. This is a continuation of the principle laid down by the South Africa Act itself[1] that membership of Parliament should be restricted to 'British subjects of European descent', but this restriction is surely very anomalous when the Africans are being represented separately from the Europeans. Twice only has this principle of restricting membership of higher[2] legislative bodies to Europeans only been waived, and in both cases the concession has been withdrawn. Up to 1956 a person qualified to be registered as a voter in the Cape Province was qualified to be chosen as a provincial councillor, irrespective of race or colour, and in terms of this law an African, the Rev. W. Rubusana, and a coloured man, Dr. Abdurahman, sat as members of the Cape Provincial Council. When Africans were put on a separate roll, they were at the same time restricted to representation in the Cape Provincial Council by Europeans only.[3] When the first Separate Representation of Voters Act—the Act subsequently declared invalid by the Supreme Court—was passed in 1951, the right of a coloured man to be elected on the Cape Provincial Council was preserved,[4] but this was taken away by a subsequent Act of 1956,[5] after the validating of the original Act by a joint sitting of both Houses of Parliament.[6] By the Asiatic Land Tenure and Indian Representation Act (No. 28 of 1946), the two members to be elected to the Natal Provincial Council to represent Indians might themselves be Indians, but this provision was repealed by Act 47 of 1948 without ever having come into force.

To meet the criticism that non-Europeans were not allowed to represent their own people in Parliament, various advisory bodies have been set up from time to time. The most important

[1] Secs. 26(d) and 44(e).
[2] In the Cape and Natal, non-Europeans may in certain circumstances be elected to municipal councils. Coloured councillors have sat on more than one Cape municipality, and an Indian—one of the few still on the Indian municipal voters' roll—in the Town Council of Stanger, Natal.
[3] Act 12 of 1936, sec. 19.   [4] Act 46 of 1951, sec. 12,
[5] Act 30 of 1956.   [6] Act 9 of 1956.

of these was the statutory Natives Representative Council set up under Act 12 of 1936,[1] and finally abolished by Act 68 of 1951. This Council consisted of the Secretary for Native Affairs as Chairman, and four nominated and twelve elected members. For the purpose of choosing this Council, the Union was divided into the same four areas as for choosing senators, namely:

  (i) the Transkeian Territories;
 (ii) the rest of the Cape Province;
(iii) Natal;
(iv) the Transvaal and the Orange Free State combined.

From each of these four areas one member was nominated by the Governor-General and three were elected. The three from the Transkeian Territories were elected by the African members of the Transkeian Territories General Council. In each of the other three areas, one member was elected by the municipal Native advisory boards to represent the urban Africans and the other two members by the remaining three categories of voting units used for the election of senators and described earlier in this chapter (local councils,[2] chiefs, and *ad hoc* electoral committees), and the method of nomination and election was *mutatis mutandis* the same as described earlier for senators. The Chief Native Commissioners of the Union sat as assessor members.

Each Council lasted for five years. Its functions were essentially advisory, but legislation 'specially affecting the interests of Natives' and annual estimates of the revenue and expenditure of the South African Native Trust Fund had to be laid before it.

The earlier meetings of the Council were constructive and the Council appeared to those who followed its proceedings to have a real if limited value, but frustration soon set in, partly avoidable by greater promptness in meeting reasonable and moderate representations made;[3] partly unavoidable, as a natural result of the strong tides of democracy, nationalism, and anti-colonialism in Africa and Asia resulting from the Second World War. In 1946 the Council passed a resolution

---

[1] Especially secs. 20-9.

[2] Or, now, Regional Bantu Authorities under Act 68 of 1951 when those have replaced local councils.

[3] One councillor likened the proceedings to 'speaking into a toy telephone'.

refusing to proceed with its agenda until the government should abolish all discriminatory legislation in South Africa. The Council met in 1947 and 1948, only to repeat this demand. After 1948 it was not called together again and it was abolished by Act 68 of 1951.

It is true that the Council had succeeded in making itself impossible, but it is equally true that no serious attempt had been made to meet its sentiments while there was still time, and perhaps it had no real place in South Africa as South Africa was developing.

Ample provision is made for tribal or semi-tribal Bantu Authorities under Act 68 of 1951, but the only attempt to provide for any quasi-representative body on a national basis is a re-enactment under section 15 of that Act of a provision of Act 23 of 1920, whereby the Governor-General may convene 'a conference of natives in the Union or any part thereof'. Up to the time of writing, no national conference has been summoned since the demise of the Natives Representative Council, though several conferences under Act 23 of 1920 were called between 1920 and 1936.

Thus not only have the Africans lost such rights as they had to be registered as voters on the common roll, but even such indirect influence as they could exert through national meetings of an advisory nature has gone into abeyance. Moreover the permanence of the present form of parliamentary representation is uncertain. It is in no way legally entrenched and more than once its abolition has been threatened. When senators or members representing Africans have gone beyond the bounds of the most tactful moderation in stating their case, indignant government members of their House have repeatedly warned them of the danger of their posts being abolished.

By the Asiatic Land Tenure and Indian Representations Act, No. 28 of 1946, it was proposed to give to Indians in the provinces of Natal and the Transvaal one elected representative in the Senate, two in the House of Assembly, and two (who might themselves be Indians) in the Natal Provincial Council. In addition, one senator was to be nominated to represent them. The Cape Indians were to remain on the common voters' roll and the very few Indians in the Orange Free State were not enfranchised at all.

The qualifications for Indian voters in the Transvaal and Natal were the passing of Standard 6 (or, for the first year of registration, Standard 4) and the possession of an income of not less than £84 per annum, or of immovable property to the value of not less than £250. This franchise was to be confined to males.

These provisions never came into effect. The Act as a whole (it must be remembered that its more important half imposed restrictions on Indian land purchase and occupation) was met with sustained protest and a passive-resistance campaign on the part of the Indians, and Indian leaders made it clear that they would not carry out the franchise provisions of the Act. These had been opposed, for very different reasons, by the Nationalist Party, and as soon as it attained power the franchise provisions of the Act were abolished by Act 47 of 1948.

No attempt has been made to set up any national advisory council for Indians.

General Hertzog's legislation of 1936 did not affect the position of the Cape and Natal coloured voters, who were left on the common roll after the Cape African voters were removed from it. An attempt by General Hertzog to grant a very limited separate coloured franchise in the Transvaal and the Orange Free State was frustrated. The Nationalist Party made the placing of Cape Coloured voters on a separate roll a major plank of its policy, and in 1951 passed through Parliament the Separate Representation of Voters Act (No. 46 of 1951). This Act was held to be invalid by the Supreme Court in 1952 (*Harris* v. *Dönges*) owing to its not having been passed according to the procedure laid down in the South Africa Act,[1] and a prolonged constitutional struggle followed, in the course of which an attempt was made to set up a rather absurd 'High Court of Parliament', the two Houses sitting as an alleged 'Law Court'. This device was unacceptable to the courts (see the further case of *Harris* v. *Dönges*).[2] The reconstitution of the Senate ultimately provided the government with a majority sufficient to enable it to meet the requirements of the South Africa Act, and in 1956 two statutes were passed by Parliament, one validating the Act of 1951 and one amending it. On the

[1] 1952 (2) S.A. 428.   [2] 1952 (4) S.A. 769.

basis of this legislation, which the Supreme Court has pronounced valid, the position of the coloured franchise is as laid down in the succeeding paragraphs.

Coloured men in the Transvaal and the Orange Free State remain completely unenfranchised.

Coloured voters registered at the time of the passing of Act 9 of 1956 in Natal remain enfranchised as long as they possess the qualifications laid down by law, but no new coloured voters may qualify, not even on a separate roll.[1]

In the Cape Province all coloured men (but no women) over the age of 21 and not disqualified by any provision of law may be registered on the Cape Coloured Voters' List if they possess the qualifications which at one time were laid down for all voters in the Cape Colony, namely, occupation for twelve months of property to the value of £75 or receipt for twelve months of salary or wages at the rate of not less than £50 and in addition ability to sign their name and write their address and occupation. Though the term 'Cape Coloured Voters' List' is used, the definitions of the Act include Indians in the Cape Province who have also been removed from the general voters' roll and put on the Cape Coloured Voters' List.

The persons on this list elect four members of the House of Assembly and two of the Cape Provincial Council, all of whom must be Europeans. In addition, the Governor-General nominates one additional senator 'on the ground of his thorough acquaintance, by reason of his official experience or otherwise, with the reasonable wants and wishes of the non-European population in the province of the Cape of Good Hope'.

Act 30 of 1956 provides for the creation of a Union Council for Coloured Affairs consisting of twelve elected and fifteen nominated non-Europeans. The elected members are chosen in and from the Cape Province, but of the nominated members two are to be chosen from Natal, one from the Orange Free State, and four from the Transvaal. Certain European officials may attend and speak at the meetings of the Council but they may not vote. The chairman is to be chosen by the members from among themselves,[2] and he will also preside over the

[1] This appears to be the effect of Act 46 of 1951, sec. 13.
[2] But in his absence the (European) Commissioner for Coloured Affairs acts as chairman (see Act 30 of 1956, sec. 14(8)).

executive committee of five members of the Council, two of whom are to be elected by their fellow-members and three nominated by the Governor-General. The tenure of office is five years and the functions of the Council are purely advisory.

The original provisions for this Council are to be found in Act 46 of 1951. There it is termed the 'Board for Coloured Affairs'. It was to have consisted of three nominated and eight elected members. The later Act reverses the position and puts nominated members in the majority.

The Council has behind it the history of a non-statutory body, the Coloured Advisory Council, set up on an experimental basis for two years in 1943 and extended by two-year periods until March 1949, before which date it had fallen into desuetude. It consisted of twenty members, all nominated, but of course the franchise on the common roll still existed. The creation of this council led to very violent opposition on the part of a large section of the coloured community, since it was regarded as the thin end of the wedge to segregate the coloured people on racial lines. It may be that similar reactions will greet the election of members for the Council for Coloured Affairs. The earlier council was also purely advisory.

In Natal and the Cape there are vestiges of older and more liberal franchise arrangements in the municipalities. Coloured persons already registered as municipal voters may remain on the roll in Natal, as may Indian voters so registered before 1924, provided that they retain their qualification. A movement is afoot to make it possible for new coloured voters in Natal to be added as they qualify. In the Cape there are some non-Europeans of all groups still registered as municipal voters. These are in the present situation anomalies.

The law relating to the parliamentary (and with it the provincial) franchise can be summed up as follows:

(1) No non-Europeans possess any vote of any kind in the Transvaal and the Orange Free State, except that chiefs, local councils, etc., return one European senator for the two provinces combined.

(2) In Natal, except for the fact that existing coloured voters remain on the roll while they retain their qualification, the position is the same in the Transvaal and the Orange Free

State. The Africans, through their chiefs, local councils, etc., return one European senator.

(3) In the Cape, voters who are not Europeans are enrolled on (*a*) a Native roll, and (*b*) a non-European (that is, coloured and Indian) roll, returning respectively three and four members to the House of Assembly and two members each to the Provincial Council. Two senators are elected to represent the Africans and one is nominated to represent coloured and Indians.

(4) All the representatives in Parliament and the Cape Provincial Council alike must be Europeans.

Thus the representation of non-Europeans is everywhere separate from that of Europeans. Moreover, it is manifestly inadequate. In the House of Assembly the representatives of Africans, coloured, and Indians, when the Separate Representation of Voters Act takes effect, will number seven out of one hundred and sixty-three, and the elected representatives of Africans in the Senate (there are no elected representatives of other non-Europeans) four out of ninety.

Moreover, this representation has the character not of a too-limited national representation but rather of a somewhat anomalous survival of ancient freedom in the Cape, particularly as the old qualifications remain and the Cape is the only province represented in the House of Assembly and even has two of the four elective seats in the Senate.

Finally, there is an air of impermanence over it all, for all legal entrenchment has been swept away, and members, as has been stated earlier, have repeatedly been threatened with abolition of office when they have raised their voices too strongly on behalf of their constituents.

What constitutional means for redress of grievances are available to the different non-European groups?

For the Indians, virtually none at all.[1]

For the Africans, a very small elected representation in the Senate and the House of Assembly.

---

[1] Except that in the Cape they are included on the Coloured Voters' List and may take their share in voting for the four elected representatives in the House of Assembly. The Cape Indians, however, form a minority on the Coloured Voters' List and a very small minority of the total Indian population, the bulk of which lives in the Transvaal and Natal.

For the coloured people, four elected representatives in the House of Assembly (but no elected member in the Senate) plus the Union Council for Coloured Affairs, the majority of whose members will be government nominees.

In view of the very stringent restrictions on the right of public meeting, free speech, and political association detailed in earlier chapters, the choice of effective extra-parliamentary action is severely limited. In Parliament the present representation can only produce results if political parties are so evenly divided and so inimical to one another that the representatives of the non-Europeans hold the balance of power and can exact concessions as the price of their support.

The right to vote is very closely bound up with civil liberty. That fact is the justification for the inclusion of a study of the franchise in the present volume. The only legal way of waging the battle for civil liberty open to non-Europeans is through their ridiculously inadequate representation in Parliament. If it is desired (and all good South Africans should desire it) that the non-Europeans should work on constitutional lines, within the law and without violence, it is imperative that more effective methods of constitutional expression of their wishes and aspirations should be made available to them.

Much more could be said, for the present separate and very limited franchise is not really defensible from any point of view, but it is desired to present the facts of the case in this volume in as objective a way as possible, and severe restraint must be exercised on comment and argument if this is to be done.

CHAPTER XII

The Administration of Native Affairs with special reference to the Reserves

On 23 June 1849, the Lieutenant-Governor of Natal issued a proclamation taking to himself the powers of Supreme Chief over all Africans residing in what was then the District, and subsequently became the Colony, of Natal.

This step was the culminating point of a four-year controversy, and was taken on the insistent advice of Theophilus Shepstone, 'Diplomatic Agent to the Native Tribes' and subsequently Secretary for Native Affairs, in the District of Natal.

The circumstances of Natal at that date were such as to make the task of the administrator of Native Affairs very difficult. Within a short period the African population had increased from approximately 25,000 to approximately 100,000 while the small European population had suffered an absolute diminution owing to the departure of many of the Voortrekkers for the north. The government had very meagre financial resources, and had been expressly discouraged by the Secretary of State for the Colonies from expecting any substantial monetary aid from Britain. Apart from the small garrison of British regular troops, whom it was thought not desirable to use for police purposes except in case of real emergency, the Secretary for Native Affairs had no real force at his disposal to compel obedience to the laws.

The historical evidence shows that the young Theophilus Shepstone, perhaps the most skilful administrator of tribal Africans ever to hold office in southern Africa, was not wedded to any conservative views in administration, and believed in early and active civilizing efforts. Hampered by lack of men and of money he fell back on 'indirect rule' as a practical method of meeting real difficulties.

Since most of the Zulu-speaking population of Natal had

been, before the European settlement, under the rule of despotic supreme chiefs, Shaka and Dingane, whose successor now reigned over the area north and east of the boundary of Natal known as Zululand, Shepstone thought that the best way of regularizing the power of the Lieutenant-Governor (and thus of himself) was to employ the conception of 'Supreme Chief'. There is no evidence to show that there had ever been a supreme chief of the Zulu-speaking peoples before the days of Shaka (1783?–1828) nor that the powers of their ordinary chiefs had been despotic. It is as though a liberal-minded Asian conqueror of Europe had proclaimed himself 'Fuehrer' on the supposition that Hitler was the normal type of European ruler.

As the years went by, and Shepstone became more and more famous for the way in which his 'system' maintained peace and order in Natal, he began to believe in it himself as a system, but his kindly and understanding personality served as a check on what in principle was legalized despotism. After he retired from office, and particularly after his death, the system in Natal become almost sacrosanct, something—to quote Burke on the British Constitution—'to be venerated where we are not presently able to comprehend'.

The powers of the Supreme Chief, defined at an early date, received further definition in the Natal Native Code of 1878, and in more imperative legal form in the Natal Native Code of 1891 (Law 19 of 1891, Natal). Similar powers were granted to the Governor of the Transvaal, and by Law 3 of 1885 (Transvaal) taken over by the State President, but not clearly enough defined.

When for the first time the Union Parliament passed a law laying down the general framework of Native administration in the Union, it confirmed in a modern and industrialized Natal, confirmed and clarified in a still more heavily industrialized Transvaal, and extended to a considerably detribalized Orange Free State, a policy adopted as a temporary expedient in the primitive conditions of a very different Natal in 1849. Section 1 of Act 38 of 1927 (as amended by Act 9 of 1929) reads:

The Governor-General shall be the Supreme Chief of all Natives in the Provinces of Natal, Transvaal and Orange Free State, and shall in any part of the said Provinces be vested with all such rights, immunities, powers and authorities in respect of all Natives as are or may be from time to time vested in him in respect of Natives in the Province of Natal.

These powers were at the time of the passing of the Acts of 1927 and 1929 defined in Chapter II of the Natal Native Code (Law 19 of 1891, Natal). But by section 24(1) of Act 38 of 1927 the Governor-General is given power 'from time to time by Proclamation in the *Gazette* to amend the provisions of the Natal Code of Native Law'. Under this authority, the Natal Code was re-enacted as a whole in amended form by Proclamation No. 168 of 1932, Chapter II of which, apart from minor amendments, contains the present-day list of the Supreme Chief's powers, authorities, rights, and immunities. It is to be noted that the Supreme Chief may, by virtue of section 24(1) of Act 38 of 1927, define and extend his own powers without any limits, and that without going to Parliament. He may also further restrict the power of the courts to interfere in any of the Supreme Chief's Acts.[1] Here is, therefore, an immense field of administrative despotism (that it is sometimes benevolent despotism does not affect the argument) completely withdrawn from the jurisdiction of the courts. Note, too, that extended powers may be given in the Transvaal and the Orange Free State by the ingenious but hardly ingenuous method of amending what is in essentials a code of tribal civil law for the Province of Natal.

The legislation of 1927 and 1929 did not apply to the Cape Province. Despite the continued existence of tribalism in the Transkeian Territories and in those northern districts which once formed the Crown Colony of 'British Bechuanaland', the Cape had for nearly a century fostered direct rather than indirect government, discouraged tribalism and given the franchise on an individual basis to thousands of Africans. Some were almost completely free from tribal ties. The Cape had never experienced the rule of a military despot such as Shaka, nor had its people ever been ruled by a single paramount chief. However, by a simple amendment contained in section 2 of Act 42 of 1956, the powers of the Governor-General as Supreme Chief were extended to 'all Natives in any part of the Union'

[1] See *Mhlingwa* v. *Secretary for Native Affairs*, 1952 (1) S.A. 312.

and thus the Cape was at last brought into line with the more authoritarian northern provinces.

What are the powers of the Supreme Chief as they affect the individual? The following extracts from the Code are relevant:

2. (The powers of the Supreme Chief shall) include the following:

(a) Power to call upon chiefs personally to render military or other service and to supply armed men or levies for the suppression of disorder and rebellion.

(b) Authority in the exercise of his functions and powers to punish disobedience of his orders or disregard of his authority by fine or imprisonment or by both fine and imprisonment.

. . . 3(1) The orders and directions of the Supreme Chief may be carried into execution by the Secretary for Native Affairs, the Chief Native Commissioner, any Native Commissioner or any other officer duly authorized by the Supreme Chief or by the Minister of Native Affairs. Any such person in carrying out such orders and directions shall be regarded as the deputy or representative of the Supreme Chief.

. . . 5(1) The Supreme Chief, the Minister of Native Affairs, the Secretary for Native Affairs, the Chief Native Commissioner, and Native Commissioners may command the attendance of Chiefs and Natives for any purpose of public interest, public utility, or for the purpose of carrying out the administration of any law, at any reasonable time and under reasonable circumstances, and in pursuance of any such purpose may require them to render obedience, assistance, and active co-operation in the execution of any reasonable order.

(2) Disregard or defiance of any order made under the provisions of sub-section (1) shall be deemed to be disregard or defiance of an order of the Supreme Chief, and any Native guilty thereof or showing disrespect to any officer referred to in sub-section (1) shall be guilty of an offence.

(3) When any such offence as is in sub-section (2) referred to is committed under circumstances rendering prompt action necessary, any such officer as is specified in sub-section (1) may order the immediate arrest of the offender and call upon him to show cause why he should not be punished. Should he fail to furnish a satisfactory explanation such officer may summarily punish the offender by a fine not exceeding ten pounds or by imprisonment for a period not exceeding two months.

. . . 8. Whenever the Supreme Chief is satisfied that any Native is dangerous to the public peace, if left at large, he may by proclamation authorize the summary arrest and detention of such Native in such place and subject to such conditions as he may determine; provided that any Native so arrested and detained may after the lapse of three months from the date of his arrest apply to the Supreme Court for his release, which shall thereupon be granted by the said Court unless such person shall then be detained under lawful warrant other than such proclamation.

. . . 10(1) Neither the Supreme Court nor any other court of law shall have jurisdiction to question and pronounce upon the validity or legality of any act done, direction or order given or punishment inflicted by the Supreme Chief in the exercise of his powers, authorities, functions, rights, immunities and privileges.

(2) No interdict or other legal process shall issue for the stay of any administrative act or order of any officer acting as the representative or deputy of the Supreme Chief or requiring any such officer to answer any suit or proceedings in respect of any such act or order unless the court be satisfied that prima facie the act or order is without lawful authority.[1]

We see thus that, theoretically, all Africans not specially exempted, practically, all Africans in the Reserves,[2] are placed under a system of legalized despotism without the right of appeal to the courts. These tremendous powers are themselves contained not in an Act of Parliament but in a proclamation, and we have now to pass on to consider the system whereby not all Africans even in theory but all Africans living in Reserves ('scheduled Native areas') may be governed on all or any matters by proclamation. Thus the administration of the Reserves is withdrawn to a very large extent from both the courts and Parliament and left in the hands of senior civil servants, disrespect to whom may, as has just been shown, be treated as disrespect to the Supreme Chief and punished accordingly.

By section 25 of the Native Administration Act (No. 38 of 1927) the Governor-General may repeal or amend any law or make, repeal or amend new laws, in so far as these are applicable to scheduled Native areas (Reserves).

The system of legislation by proclamation for Reserves has a

---

[1] Proclamation 168 of 1932, secs. 2, 3, 5, 8, and 10.
[2] In practice the sections of the Code quoted are not applied outside the Reserves. Africans in urban areas have other restrictions but not these. For the partial system of exemption, see later in this chapter.

long history, even in the Cape with its liberal parliamentary tradition; there is much to be said for it, and much has been said in its defence in past years. It is, however, liable to abuse, and an examination of some of the proclamations issued will reveal the fact that much that is unreasonable and tyrannical can happen under the system. Before proceeding to this, it is advisable to examine briefly the safeguards which Parliament has inserted in the relevant sections of the Native Administration Act. They are three in number, (a) the proclamation must normally have been published in the *Gazette* for at least one month before it is finally promulgated;[1] (b) every Proclamation shall be laid upon the tables of both Houses of Parliament within fourteen days after its promulgation if Parliament is in ordinary session, or otherwise within fourteen days after the commencement of the next ensuing session, and if both Houses of Parliament by resolutions passed in the same session request the Governor-General to repeal or modify a proclamation, he shall forthwith repeal or modify it by a further proclamation in the *Gazette*;[2] (c) if the Native Affairs Commission should dissent from any provision contained in a proclamation, this dissent and the reasons for it shall be laid upon the tables of both Houses of Parliament simultaneously with the proclamation.

The first of these safeguards is of very limited value in practice, although in theory educated Africans and their friends should in a systematic way watch the *Gazette* and protest while there is time. Few people other than officials and business men, scarcely any Africans, do in fact read the *Gazette* regularly, and a month in a country of great distances is a very short time to organize protests or make representations.

The reviewing functions of Parliament are exercised by sessional committees of both Houses. Like all other sessional committees, these are so constituted as to reflect the proportion of parties in each House. The Minister of Native Affairs would not be in office did his party not command a majority of the House of Assembly, and since the Senate Act of 1955, it has been all but impossible to have a Senate of a different party

---

[1] Act 38 of 1927, sec. 25(2).   [2] Act 38 of 1927, sec. 26(1) and (2).

composition from that of the House.[1] Thus both sessional committees normally have majorities supporting the Minister who
is virtually—though the Governor-General is the formal
signatory to them—the author of the proclamations. Moreover
the debates taking place in the sessional committees are not
published, but only the resolutions, so that report after report
includes only the approval of every proclamation submitted.
Perhaps the best comment on the efficacy of the system is that
during thirty years there has not been a single instance of
Parliament exercising its right to demand repeal or modification
of a proclamation.

The third safeguard may perhaps strike one as being a very
useful one, but this depends on the composition of the Native
Affairs Commission. From its inception the constitution of the
Commission permitted, curiously enough, the nomination of a
sitting member of Parliament and provided that the membership of the Commission should not constitute 'an office of
profit under the Crown',[2] so that any senator or member of the
House of Assembly nominated thereto would not be disqualified
as a member of Parliament. The first Commission consisted of
two extra-parliamentary members and only one parliamentary
member, but at the time of writing the Commission is made up
of one extra-parliamentary member and four parliamentary
members, all avowed supporters of the government of the day.
Such a body can hardly be expected to report adversely to
Parliament over the head of the Minister on one of his own
proclamations.

Together with proclamations must be taken regulations
published under Government Notice, which are also habitually
submitted to the sessional committees on Native Affairs.

Let us examine some of the legislation contained in these
instruments. By Proclamation 252 of 1928 the holding in any
Reserve[3] of 'gatherings or assemblies of natives in excess of ten
in number' was prohibited with certain exceptions. Government

---

[1] For a few months in 1948–9 the Senate did have a majority of one vote against
the government; this is the only exception in recent decades.

[2] Act 23 of 1920, sec. 1.

[3] The actual wording is 'any Native location, reserve or mission reserve in
Natal, the Transvaal and the Orange Free State'. The prohibition has been
subsequently extended to the Cape.

10

Notice 2017 of 18 September 1953[1] extended this prohibition to urban areas. The exceptions include bona fide religious services;[2] meetings held by representatives of the Africans in the Senate, the House of Assembly, or the Cape Provincial Council, or by candidates for such posts; bona fide sports gatherings, concerts, or entertainments. They also happily include weddings and funerals. But the general and fundamental right of public meeting, one of the most elementary of civil liberties, has been slain; and, as if to add insult to injury, not by parliamentary statute, but by the hands of meaner executioners—proclamations and Government Notices.

The right of Europeans to visit the Reserves has also been terminated by legislation.[3] Europeans may pass through the Reserves as travellers, but they may not pay visits there without the permission of the Native commissioner concerned. Enacted with the intention of hampering the movement in the Reserves of liquor-peddlers, communist agitators and other persons whom the government thought undesirable, the prohibition has never been applied systematically, but in its sporadic application it has been used to control the movements of missionaries, teachers, bona fide students of language and anthropology, and sometimes scientists. It is part of the general set-up which seeks by means of State action to keep the races separate and to prevent social contacts.

It is noteworthy that the earlier proclamation on public meetings was enacted as far back as 1928 and not as part of the recent wave of apartheid laws.

In the Reserves the administration is increasingly based on the tribal system, even in areas where for long periods in the past this was systematically discouraged. The unit of administration under the Native commissioner, who is always a white man, is the chief. The term *chief* requires examination. It may denote the paramount ruler of a large ethnic group comprising hundreds of thousands of people; it may mean the head of a little knot of a few score of families. A chief may be the hereditary ruler of a people, whose ancestry, lovingly preserved in tribal lore, goes back many generations; he may be the

[1] Amended by Government Notice 1074 of 4 June 1954.
[2] Now however subject to certain other restrictions (see Chapter IX).
[3] Act 18 of 1936, sec. 24(1).

descendant of some commoner who was exalted to chieftainship by the white man's government a century ago or less; he may be a government nominee, either a member of the royal line who is not the direct heir or (in very rare cases) a commoner. But influential or insignificant, aristocrat or parvenu, he is, whatever else he may be, a government servant. As such he must obey orders or imperil his position. Chiefs have been deposed in our own day for disobeying government orders or even for taking political action of which the government does not approve. It is true that such action is less likely to be taken against powerful hereditary paramount chiefs whose deposition would create widespread dissatisfaction, perhaps even resistance, than against lesser tribal heads, but all are in the same position fundamentally. They cannot protect their status by faithfully obeying the law. That is not enough. It is *persons* whom they have to obey: to be law-abiding will not save them if they run counter to Government policy or hurt the pride of some Minister or official. As chiefs they are not under the rule of law, but rather the rule of men.

This is the more disturbing when one realizes that it is almost solely through the chiefs today that the Native Affairs Department can keep in touch with African opinion and test African reactions. The new 'Bantu authorities' (whose composition and functions will be discussed shortly) are grouped round the chiefs, and a sustained effort is being made to set up these authorities in place of the partly elected local and general councils. A chief needs great courage to oppose the government's policy on a single point, and a valour bordering on foolhardiness to criticize its policy as a whole. Hence the little candle of democracy that might otherwise shine through the ancient tribal institutions is concealed under a bushel of self-protecting caution.

A chief stands often between two perils. If he never protests against policies which his people hate, his influence diminishes and he may even be despised: if he raises his voice in opposition he may be deposed. As a voter he may vote for a senator opposed to government policy, but should he be too enthusiastic in the support of his chosen candidate, or if that candidate, having been elected, is too forthright in opposition to the government, there may well be repercussions. He is like a school prefect placed between a school seething with discontent and a suspicious and arbitrary headmaster.

The 'Bantu authorities' set up under Act 68 of 1951 are of three grades—tribal, regional, and territorial—but in all cases they are based on the chief and on tribal organization. Members of a regional authority, for example, are 'elected or selected' from 'amongst the chiefs, headmen and councillors of the tribal authorities for the areas in respect of which such regional authority is established'.[1] The appointment of any councillor or any member of a regional or territorial authority may be cancelled, after due inquiry 'held by an officer of the public service appointed by the Minister for that purpose', if the Minister is satisfied that the removal of such councillor or member . . . 'is desirable in the general interest of natives' in the area.[2] A Bantu authority may make by-laws falling within its terms of jurisdiction under the Act, but 'no such by-law shall have any force or effect until it has been approved by the Governor-General . . . and the Governor-General may, before approving of any by-law, refer it back to the authority concerned for consideration and thereafter amend it in such manner as he may deem fit or make additional by-laws or amend or repeal any existing by-law'.[3] A by-law so amended 'shall be deemed to have been duly made in the amended form by the regional authority concerned'.[4] The method of election or selection of members and their periods and conditions of office are prescribed not by statute but by regulation in the Governor-General's discretion.[5]

The most recent regulations affecting these bodies are to be found in Government Notice No. 1178 of 2 August 1957. Under these regulations, the chairman of a regional authority shall always be a chief should a chief be available.[6] No member shall use 'offensive or unbecoming words' in reference to any officer of the government or any member or *employee* of the regional authority.[7] It is for the chairman to decide whether 'offensive or unbecoming' words have been used, and it is he

---

[1] Act 68 of 1951, sec. 3(3).   [2] Ib., sec. 3(4).
[3] Ib., sec. 5(2).   [4] Ib., sec. 5(3).
[5] Ib., sec. 17.
[6] Government Notice 1178 of 2 August 1957, para. 3(1).
[7] Government Notice 1178 of 2 August 1957, para. 21. The italics are ours.

who, if the member refuses to withdraw and apologize, or if
he repeats his offence, may suspend him and order his removal,
and he 'may call on any native policeman or tribal policeman
or any other native there present to effect his removal'. In such
circumstances, opposition is surely bound to be decorous! The
general public are excluded from meetings, unless they are
members of the tribe concerned, except with the approval of
the Native commissioner.[1] The regulation is so drawn up as to
prevent the elected parliamentary representative of the people
concerned from being present without the Native Commissioner's authorization.

It is undoubtedly the intention of the government to build
up the system of Bantu authorities into a real organ of local
government in the Reserves; but the steed is kept on a short
rein with bit and bridle, and one is left with the impression
that at all times executive authority in the person of the Native
Affairs Department must have virtually unlimited control, to
the exclusion of both Parliament and the courts. There are no
points of importance governed by law enforceable in the
courts and overriding administrative orders.

This is the case also with one of the most important economic
aspects of life in the Reserves, namely, the allocation of land,
which is the task of the chief, subject to appeal to the Native
commissioner. There are many practical arguments for leaving
this matter in the ordinary way to administrative discretion
(for which reason we do not propose to make an issue of it),
but injustice is possible and here again no appeal to the courts
is possible.

The Native Administration Act of 1927 provides for letters
of exemption exempting the recipient from certain laws
affecting Africans.[2] But this exemption, unlike that granted by
Law 28 of 1865 (Natal) on which it was based, is in every
respect a matter of administrative discretion. The Natal Law
indeed left it to the discretion of the Governor whether exemption was to be granted or not, but the nature of the exemption
was specified in the Law. Not so in the Act of 1927. In this the
Governor-General may grant a letter 'exempting the recipient
from such laws, specially affecting natives, or so much of such

[1] Ib., para. 30.   [2] Act 38 of 1927, sec. 31.

laws as may be specified in such letter, provided that no such exemption shall be granted . . . from any provision of law regulating the ownership or occupation of land, or imposing taxation or controlling the sale, supply or possession of intoxicating liquor'. Any exemption may be made 'subject to any conditions imposed by the Governor-General'. Any letter of exemption may 'at any time be cancelled by the Governor-General without assigning any reason'. Thus there is no degree of civilization which will legally entitle an African to be treated as if he were a European, or even to be exempted as of right from a certain number of clearly specified differentiating statutes; though exemption does in practice give a measure of relief to a certain number of people, but on a discretionary, and therefore to some extent a precarious, basis.[1]

Before proceeding to sum up the position, it may be as well to draw attention to the continuous process of delegation which is going on from higher to lower authorities. Thus, to take a few examples out of many, functions originally entrusted in the Native Administration Act of 1927 to the Governor-General have been delegated to the Minister of Native Affairs,[2] functions entrusted to the Minister have been delegated to the Secretary or Under-Secretary for Native Affairs,[3] functions entrusted to the Under-Secretary have been delegated to the Chief Native Commissioner.[4] Functions entrusted by the Native Taxation and Development Act to the Minister of Native Affairs have been delegated to the Secretary,[5] while functions entrusted by the Native Trust and Land Act to the Minister may be delegated to 'any member of the Native Affairs Commission, the Secretary for Native Affairs *or any other officer of the Department of Native Affairs*'.[6]

The facts assembled in this chapter and elsewhere in this book indicate that the Native Affairs Department has gradually

---

[1] The question of exemption raises the whole question of 'Native Law' codified in Natal, uncodified in the other provinces and of formal exemption from it in Natal, and the more flexible recognition of degrees of civilization by the courts in the other provinces; also the question of the 'exemption' or 'emancipation' of women from their position of tutelage in Native Law. But this, though a fascinating subject of study and of immense and sometimes poignant importance, is hardly 'civil liberties'!

[2] Act 56 of 1949, secs. 22 and 24.   [3] Ib., sec. 23.

[4] Ib., sec. 19.   [5] Ib., sec. 18.

[6] Act 79 of 1957, sec. 5.

become an *imperium in imperio*. From the administration of the Reserves both Parliament and the Supreme Court are virtually excluded; and the same statement holds good for vast and increasing fields of African life outside the Reserves. It is most important not to exaggerate the position, nor to use polemical language, but it is mere sober truth to say that, almost completely in the Reserves, and to an increasing extent outside them, the African does not enjoy the benefits of the rule of law; that almost completely in the Reserves[1] and to an increasing extent outside them, he has no rights against the government and no real civil liberty. The Native administration of South Africa is to an increasing extent legalized despotism. It is sometimes benevolent despotism, but always despotism. Official discretion has increasingly replaced legal rights. Such a state of affairs is incongruous in a State which still claims to be a democracy and to be subject in some measure to the rule of law. That the bureaucratic despotism of the Native Affairs Department should help to create an atmosphere in which the rights of other sections of the community give place steadily, if still only in part, to the rule of Ministers and public servants to a state of affairs in which official discretion encroaches quietly and steadily on the rule of law—is, after all, not surprising. The battle for the rights of white South Africans has largely been lost in advance by the lack of care for the rights of black South Africans.

[1] See e.g., *Rex* v. *Nqwabeni,* 1952 (4) S.A. 53; *Rex* v. *Kumalo,* 1949 (1) S.A. 513.

CHAPTER XIII

Conclusions

In the main this book has been a recital of facts, with a minimum of comment. Comment would only have got in the way. The accumulation of the facts is more impressive than anything else could be. As restriction is piled upon restriction, one is deeply moved at the picture which is disclosed. Even to those used to these conditions, the effect of marshalling them in order is devastating: the heart seeks almost desperately for some ray of hope, some dawn of freedom.

All this has happened in a country with a great tradition of liberty. The very men responsible for the restrictive legislation are the descendants of those who left the known things of life for the unknown wilderness in order to be free. How can it be that such men have surrendered freedom for others, and in the process for themselves?

The answer which must be abundantly clear to any careful reader of this book is that freedom has been bartered for the hope of apartheid. Is it worth it?

To many students of South African life it must seem that white South Africa is being led farther and farther into the desert, away from the cool waters of home towards a mirage which will never materialize. Even the Tomlinson Commission made it clear that, if all their drastic proposals for the development of the Reserves and the withdrawal of much African labour from European areas were carried out in full, there would still in twenty-five years' time be as many Africans in urban areas as there are today; and of course their proposals leave the coloured and Indian populations untouched. The government's practical policies of apartheid are far less drastic than those advocated by the Tomlinson Report. That non-Europeans residing outside the Reserves will be satisfied to remain indefinitely in the conditions in which they find themselves at present is incredible. That those in the Reserves will be permanently satisfied with a measure of local government is also unthinkable. Ultimately apartheid is a mirage, an elaborate form of self-deception, the object of which is to avoid the facing of unpalatable facts. It is no more than this.

It is for this will-o'-the-wisp that South Africans are being asked to give up their freedom, and in doing so to surrender one of the greatest treasures of that Western civilization of which they are proud to be the special guardians in Africa.

Freedom is thus being sacrificed in order to maintain the barriers against racial equality, to protect the young nationalism of white South Africa, and to ensure the political supremacy of the larger of the two white groups. But while this is so, there are not wanting signs that the steady process of destroying established liberties is leading many people to admire regulation and authoritarianism for its own sake. Not only because they believe in apartheid, but also because they do not very much believe in freedom, many South Africans are glorifying 'strong' government, or at least accepting without demur the cult of the political Messianism of Ministers.

It is difficult for those who have not themselves lived through the gradual establishment of a tyranny to understand the subtle dangers of the 'softening-up' process, the effect on all but very strong personalities of intimidation. Laws which would have aroused the fiercest opposition in 1947 meet with sullen acquiescence in 1957. Men feel frustrated and disheartened: opposition seems to be uniformly unsuccessful. They take for granted interventions in private life which they still dislike but to which they are becoming conditioned. And added to this is the intimidation exercised by so many laws and made more real by practical experience. Of all these laws the most intimidating is the Criminal Law Amendment Act of 1953. Referred to already earlier in this book, this Law imposes penalties on all who in any way whatever advise, encourage, or incite other people 'to commit an offence by way of protest against any law, or in support of any campaign for the repeal or modification of any law', and the maximum penalties are a fine of £500, imprisonment for five years, or a whipping of ten strokes; in the case of a second offence, the fine may not be imposed except in conjunction with a whipping or imprisonment. These savage penalties have in fact silenced many people who would otherwise have taken action, not least because they realize that the government, fearing to incur odium by imposing them on well-known and respected citizens, may easily select for arrest their less-known non-European colleagues, and that the penalties may fall on these.

It is not always easy to see what course should be followed by friends of freedom in these circumstances. But at least they must keep their own minds clear, speak the truth boldly, and protest in every constitutional way open to them. To do less would be rank disloyalty to South Africa, who needs the honesty and courage of all her sons.

For those outside South Africa there are also lessons to be learned from this study. In recent years it has been common for writers in public administration and constitutional law to attack Dicey's classical exposition of the doctrine of the rule of law. All of us must admit that some modification of it is necessary to meet the complexity of legislation and government in the Welfare State; but only those who have seen the fundamental principles of civil liberty systematically attacked can see how brightly they shine, how essentially true and sound they are. Those who treat them lightly might well ask themselves how they would really like to do without them; to those deprived of them they shine out very clearly in their night as the lost but essential light of true freedom.

The principles of freedom must be cherished for their own sakes. Some of the more extreme critics of the South African government want to overthrow it by giving the vote to all, without diminishing the excessive powers of the South African State. Thus you would have the same principles of authoritarianism exercised by a different government. But constitutional liberty is not enough. Ultra-radical authoritarianism is no more acceptable than semi-fascist authoritarianism. Whether a privileged minority or a majority holds the reins of government, the State should be limited to its proper functions, and the liberties of individuals and social groups within the body politic preserved. Constitutional liberty is a laudable end, but not to the exclusion of civil liberty.

In conclusion, let us look at the facts set forth without exaggeration or misrepresentation in this book. There is nothing like facing facts. The power of the truth is ultimately stronger than all the might of government. Justice and freedom must be defended patiently, stubbornly, without illusion and without despair, and no weapon for their defence is stronger than the sword of truth. *Magna est veritas et praevalebit.*

Index

A.

A Survey of Race Relations in South Africa, 1953-4, 56 n.; 1955-6, 56 n.
Abdurahman, Dr., 146
Act 9 of 1892 (C), 139 n.
administrative courts, 15, 16
administration of Native Affairs, 154-66
African Factory Worker, The, 90
African Methodist Episcopal Church, 123
African National Congress, 77, 82
African opinion and Native Affairs Department, 162
Afrikaans-medium schools, 110
amenities, separate, 46-7
Anglican Church, 124, 127
Anglican Church, Sophiatown, 131-2
Annual Survey of South African Law: 1954, 95; 1955, 71 n., 93
apartheid, 8, 111, 131, 168; in mission schools, 134; Nationalists' belief in, 168
Aquinas, St. Thomas, 3
Arenstein v. Durban Corporation, 1952 (1) S.A. 279 (A.D.), 82
Asiatic Land Tenure and Indian Representation Act, 28 of 1946, 9, 140, 146, 148
audi alteram partem, 62, 65

B.

banning of objectionable literature, 74
Bantu Authorities, 148, 162-3
Bantu Authorities Act, 68 of 1951, 147, 148, 163
Bantu Education Act, 47 of 1953, 109, 113, 114
Bantu education, Eiselen Commission Report on, 113, 114, 115
Bantu Prophets in South Africa, 123 n.
Bantu, traditional tribal government, 6-7
Baptist Union, 128
Batavian Republic, 5
British Constitution, 12; effect on Transvaal and Orange Free State constitutions, 3, 6
British tradition, 3, 6, 8
Brookes, 8 n., 90 n.
Bryce, 3-4
bus boycott, 40-1

C.

Cabinet Government, 72, 88
Calvinistic authoritarianism, 4
Cape Coloured voters' list, 150-2
Cape of Good Hope Constitution Ordinance, 1852, 139 n.
Cape of Good Hope, effect of British tradition on, 3
censorship, 74 ff.
Central Native Labour Board, 105
Charter of Natal, 1856, 140 n.
Christelike Nasionale Onderwys, 109 ff.
Church, generally, 2, 10; freedom of, 122-32; and educational freedom, 112-13; and social freedom, 133; veto on erection of new for Africans, 126
'Church clause', 126 ff.
C.I.D. Security Branch, 42, 86, 137; Special Branch, 41-2, 120 n., 133; *and see* Police
civil liberty defined, 1
Clayton, Most Rev. Dr. G. H., 127
Coal Mines Regulation (England), 1887, 38
Colour problems of South Africa, 8 n.
coloured, 43; classification of, 46; old-age pensions, 47; labour, 91
Coloured Advisory Council, 151
Congregational Church, 124, 128
Cost of Living for Africans, The, 99 n.
Criminal Law Amendment Act, 8 of 1953, 77-8, 168; penalties under, 168-9
Criminal Procedure Act ('Criminal Code'), 56 of 1955, 31, 32-9, 41, 45, 84
Criminal Procedure and Evidence Act, 31 of 1917, 31, 34
curfew, 55, 59
Customs Act, 55 of 1955, 74
Cyprian Bhekuzulu, 59

D.

Declaration of Rights of Man, 1
Departure from the Union Regulation Act, 34 of 1955, 61, 69-71
De Villiers, J., 72
De Villiers, Sir Henry, 26
Dicey, A. V., 12-13
Dingane, 7 n.